PRAISE FOR

"This is an important and significant book. It is well written and lucid, using a wealth of examples and stories to develop arguments in a compelling way. Its message is critical in these difficult times. It should be required reading for rationalists everywhere."
Gareth Jones, Visiting Professor IE Business School and bestselling author of Why Should Anyone Be Led By You?

"Being comfortable with leaning into your own Not Knowing is at the heart of all great leadership work today. The essence of leadership is about sensing, leaning into, and actualizing emerging future possibilities. D'Souza and Renner's book gives you a highly fascinating account on the frontline of this new leadership work."
Dr C Otto Scharmer, Senior Lecturer at the Massachusetts Institute of Technology (MIT), author of Theory U *and Founding Chair of the Presencing Institute*

"Not Knowing is a critical skill needed by leaders to tackle the complex problems we face in society. D'Souza and Renner's book gives readers the confidence to face the edges of their own expertise and to create new value by venturing into new territory."
Carsten Sudhoff, Former Chief Human Resources Officer of the World Economic Forum and Founder and CEO of Circular Society

"I love this book because it not only encourages us, but it compels us to be comfortable with Not Knowing and helps us realise that a new and exciting path can be created when we do. A must read for anyone who wants to be successful in the 21st Century and beyond."
Rebecca Miller, Head of Future Capability at National Australia Bank

"Not Knowing is being comfortable with curiosity, loving it, as we create the future we all want to be a part of. The craft of entrepreneurs is to demystify the unknown. Master storytellers Steven and Diana help us explore this fascinating world, in an erudite and engaging manner, in which we all become a part of the stories behind the people driving change."
Sherry Coutu CBE, Entrepreneur, Non-Exec Director, Investor and Advisor to companies, universities and charities

"A fascinating, insightful, reassuring and practical exploration of a critical stage that will unnerve even the most productive person. This book demystifies what all of us experience, worry about, try to avoid and yet live with. It is a must have for any person facing the unknown, dancing at the edge of discovery, wanting to break out of their existing mould. It will be recommended reading for all my leadership programmes."
Magdalena Bak-Maier PhD, Talent Coach, Leadership Development Specialist and Author of Get Productive!

"Despite our brains being programmed to search for certainty, a commonly cited proverb states that the only certain things in life is death and taxes! D'Souza and Renner's book is a vigorous, lucid and illustrative tour on the meaning of uncertainty and its implications for our private and professional lives. Destined to become a reference book for managers who aim to improve their strategic vision, the book offers valuable insights and advice on how to find equilibrium in a constantly changing and uncertain world."
Santiago Iniguez de Onzono, Dean of IE Business School

"This book is a critical guide for current and future leaders. We need our leaders of today and tomorrow to navigate and embrace the unknown in order to successfully respond to that which awaits us. Embrace the stories that are told within this work- they are powerful. Then ask yourself what is your story and your ability to lead in such a time."
Kate Harris, Chief Executive Officer at the Centre for Sustainability Leadership

"*Not Knowing* is brilliant. Renner and D'Souza condition us to accept what we know and to lean in to what we don't. Who knew Not Knowing was such a smart thing to do? I'm not vulnerable if I don't know what I or others think I need to know. Rather, "not knowing" is a gateway to more progress. This book is a helpful mix of theory and practice. It's grounded and well researched. Well done! The book helped me and I'll recommend it to others."
Ed O'Malley, President and CEO of
Kansas Leadership Center

"In an interconnected world, dealing with complexity distin guishes the great leader from the adequate manager. Future shock and tipping points lead us to "Finisterre": the edge of knowledge. Our daily life in the planet human system requires new approaches. Renner and D'Souza's work provides new insights and practical tools to guide us."
Richard Dent OAM, CEO of Leadership Victoria

"The premise that D'Souza and Renner offer is intuitively obvious, but rarely recognized and they do a terrific job of bringing it to our consciousness. It is certainty they argue against; the arrogance of believing somehow that knowledge is finite and waiting as a bride in the vestibule for us to merely get our cognitive tuxedo on. Yet all of us - even the brilliant and successful - realize it is the Unknowing that provides the inspiration for all that we do. It is so seductive to be right, even as that prospect strips our world of wonder. To read and practice what this work suggests is to shrug off habits and attitudes that keep us from the true joy of living and creating. I will keep it next to my bed."
Terry Pearce, author of Leading Out Loud
and Clicks and Mortar, *Founder and*
President of Leadership Communication

"We all need the safe and familiar but your relationship with the unknown plays a big part in determining the quality of your life. When you see the unknown as full of possibility and potential, you will allow yourself to be excited, inspired, curious, empowered and courageous. Steven and Diana's book is an invitation to your enquiry with the unknown and an opportunity to develop a new relationship with the unknown. Read and be curious."

Nick Williams, author of eight books including
The Work We Were Born To Do

"We're most comfortable and confident as leaders when the issues we face are within our level of competence; we are much less so in the unchartered waters beyond the edge of our competence. The complex and chaotic nature of our lives and work suggest that leaders will increasingly face more 'unknowns' than 'knowns.' Indeed, the capacity to engage one's self and others in addressing these unknowns may be *the* critical leadership success factor for the coming decade. This book is your valuable guide for that journey."

Dr Barry Bales, Assistant Dean at the
Lyndon B Johnson School of Public Affairs,
The University of Texas

"To a degree, certainty has always been a delusion, but no more so than today. Humans are wired to rush to solve instead of rush to discover. Paradoxically, if we are to solve the 21st Century's wicked problems, we need to embrace the unknown, to be comfortable with and appreciate it, even immerse ourselves in it, at the edges of the known. This is how we will gain insights, see opportunities, create innovations and develop relationships that lead us to the solutions. The stories in this book will give you the confidence to thrive in not knowing by learning how others have managed it. Perhaps you can add your story at the end."

Deborah Mills-Scofield LLC, Brown University
Visiting Scholar and Partner at Glengary LLP

"The well written wisdom you will find here is hard to come by in our information obsessed world. Learn from the older tradition, and learn from D'Souza and Renner who could only say it so well because they both experienced it and also learned from it."
Richard Rohr, OFM at the Center for Action and Contemplation, Albuquerque, New Mexico

"This is a rare book that moves beyond oversimplifying the complexity and ambiguity facing organisations and surfaces an instinctive but dangerous truth; it is human not to know. Renner and D'Souza encourage us to work against our hardwiring to embrace Not Knowing as a way to thrive in uncertainty rather than retreat to the false security of easy answers."
Andrew Stevens, Director, Executive Education at The University of Adelaide

"The future belongs to the learners, not the knowers. Steven and Diana are master storytellers, taking us on a journey to the edge of curiosity – Not Knowing. The people you meet in this book will become your companions and inspiration along the way."
Richard Leider, international bestselling author of The Power of Purpose, Repacking Your Bags, & Life Reimagined

"In a fast changing world, knowledge and expertise appear to offer reassurance and answers. However, Renner and D'Souza alert us to the exciting idea that, while knowledge may be power, *Not Knowing* creates a space where authentic leadership can be exercised and deep meaning can be sought."
David Sweeney, Director of Leadership at NSW Health Education and Training Institute, New South Wales Government, Australia

"In times of Not Knowing, this is the book you have to reach for; reassuring, inspiring, insightful – a true north for times of uncertainty."
Preethi Nair, author and MD of Kiss the Frog

"We don't know what our society is going to look like in 20 years' or how its economy will be organized. It needs to transform in a way that hasn't happened for centuries – and no one knows what it's going to be like. Those who lead us to this new economy will have to be able to deal positively with uncertainty. Steven and Diana's book not only gives everyone a head-start on dealing with Not Knowing, it also gives us a vocabulary and stories through which we can share our experiences."
Tom Rippin, CEO of On Purpose

"Leadership generates capacity, not dependency; and new capacity to meet adaptive challenges requires courage and permission to push beyond the frontiers of current competence. In a compelling, delightful and easy-to-read way, the authors provide essential wisdom for all who aim to increase the adaptive capacity of people around the globe."
Ronald Heifetz, MD and Founding Director of the Center for Public Leadership and King Hussein bin Talal Senior Lecturer in Public Leadership at Harvard Kennedy School

"Decades ago, Nobel laureate Werner Heisenberg said physics does not describe nature, but our current knowledge of nature. Yet, we often assume our knowledge of the world and the world are the same. It is a dangerous assumption. This book is a timely reminder that the map is not the territory and that all knowledge is provisional. We should learn to live with the uncertainty of Not Knowing, and act accordingly."
Martin Gargiulo, Professor of Organizational Behaviour at INSEAD

NEW EDITION

NOT KNOWING

THE ART OF TURNING UNCERTAINTY INTO OPPORTUNITY

STEVEN D'SOUZA

DIANA RENNER

LONDON NEW YORK SHANGHAI
MADRID BARCELONA BOGOTA
MEXICO CITY MONTERREY BUENOS AIRES

Published by

LID Publishing Ltd

One Adam Street, London WC2N 6LE

31 West 34th Street, 8th Floor, Suite 8004,
New York, NY 10001, U.S.

info@lidpublishing.com
www.lidpublishing.com

A member of:
www.businesspublishersroundtable.com

Printed in Great Britain by TJ International

ISBN: 978-1-910649-66-4

Cover design: Caroline Li
Page design: iconic.com

To our parents,
Christine and Silverio D'Souza, and Margit and Petru Gheorghiu,
whose courage leaving familiar shores and venturing into the
unknown is a constant source of inspiration.

CONTENTS

FOREWORD
BY MARSHALL GOLDSMITH

Change is an opportunity. This is the message Steven D'Souza and Diana Renner expound upon in *Not Knowing: The Art of Turning Uncertainty into Opportunity*.

As the title states, turning uncertainty into opportunity is an art. It takes a very special type of leader to manage uncertainty and turn it into a competitive advantage.

Highly successful leaders may navigate uncertainty as a matter of course. In fact, it is a natural tendency for some leaders, for instance, Apple founder Steve Jobs, who advised Stanford University graduates to "stay hungry, stay foolish", to take chances and trust that risk-taking would be fruitful, no matter the outcome.

Many, many leaders do not have this knack for leading change. One of the things that holds leaders back from turning uncertainty into opportunity is what I call "The Success Delusion".

Put simply, the success delusion is the fact that "any human, in fact, any animal will tend to repeat behaviour that is followed by positive reinforcement. The more successful we become, the more positive reinforcement we get – and the more likely we are to experience the success delusion. The idea is this: "I behave this way. I am successful. Therefore, I must be successful because I behave this way." This delusion that what we've been doing will keep working holds us back from taking chances on the unknown.

Few of us are immune to the success delusion. Overcoming it requires vigilance and constantly asking yourself if the behaviour you are exhibiting is a legitimate reason for your success, or if you are just kidding yourself.

If you don't have a knack and enthusiasm for rapidly shifting gears to pursue new opportunities or for the self-exploration you must do to make changes, read *Not Knowing* by Steven D'Souza and Diana Renner. If you do have this natural tendency, I highly recommend you read this book as well. You can expand that exceptionally valuable talent of yours by reading this work written by two people who understand the subject of change like few authors I've read.

I hope you enjoy this book as much as I did!

Life is good.

Marshall Goldsmith
Author of the #1 *New York Times* bestseller – *Triggers*

FOREWORD
BY MARTY LINSKY

It takes a certain amount of chutzpah to write a book about the virtues of Not Knowing. After all, if my friends and colleagues, Diana Renner and Steven D'Souza, want you to acknowledge your ignorance and enjoy the rewards of stepping into the unknown, how can they possibly know enough about it to write a whole book, making it comprehensible to us? How can anyone be "knowledgeable" about Not Knowing?

Nevertheless, this paradoxical quest for knowing about Not Knowing has to resonate with anyone who has been in professional life, or who has even experienced being a parent. It certainly does with me. The pressure to "know" has been present throughout my professional journey.

As a young, over-educated, under-experienced political operative, I was charged with running a big chunk of my mentor's campaign for Attorney General of Massachusetts. I had no idea what I was doing. Rather than acknowledge that to myself or my superiors, I tried to compensate by coming into the office earlier and earlier, as if somehow spending more time at the job would compensate for my ignorance. I was close to a nervous breakdown.

As a politician – an ambitious three-term-elected Massachusetts state legislator – I was expected to have the answers and to have a point of view about everything. I complied, talking authoritatively about whatever I was asked by constituents or reporters.

Then I became a journalist myself, eventually the editor of a weekly newspaper. It was my first job as a manager and, once again, I had no idea what I was doing. I had to act, to make decisions, both managerial and journalistic, and had neither the courage nor the confidence to acknowledge how much I was floundering in the Not Knowing realm and ask for help.

Finally, in my dotage, with a lot less to prove to myself or to others, I have spent the past 30 years teaching at Harvard. In that environment, where knowledge is king, I have finally been able and willing to enjoy Not Knowing and being seen as abdicating my responsibility to disseminate wisdom. The classrooms in which I teach are designed so that everyone faces the front of the room, where the professor professes, dispensing pearls of knowledge, as if the students had nothing to contribute except their deference. My best teaching, when I make the greatest contribution to the growth of my students, always comes when I enter the classroom completely empty-headed, when I am fully present and listening to them, rather than to the voices in my head that are full of teaching plans and assumed truths.

As a parent, I have experienced that wonderful and difficult moment when your child suddenly realizes that you do not know everything, that you are not infallible, and that you make mistakes on a regular basis. I remember once yelling at my middle child, my older son, probably then about 9 years old, when he was playing baseball. I was urging him to stand closer to the home plate so that he would have a better chance of hitting the pitch. He did what I said and the next pitch hit him squarely in the arm. That was more than 30 years ago and I can still see the look on his face as he ran up the first base line, in pain, holding back the tears, bewildered that he had followed my advice and that it had caused him grief. The scales had fallen from his eyes.

As a human being, functioning in organizational life, you must have experienced both the pressure on you to "Know" and the pressure you put on others, especially those in authority, to know the answers, to provide the classic functions of authority: direction, protection and order, even when they didn't have the slightest idea about what was going on.

This book, honoring and legitimizing the space of Not Knowing is the work of liberators not Luddites, freeing us to innovate, adapt, and address the complexity, ambiguity and uncertainty of life in the 21st Century with curiosity, empathy and, yes, the courage to withstand the resistance of those who desperately hold on to the illusion that current knowledge can solve the most vexing problems.

This book is a living example of that courage, that willingness to jump off the cliff into the nothingness of Not Knowing, which is so essential if we are to make progress on the most intractable challenges we face globally and in our everyday lives.

Marty Linsky
Faculty, Harvard Kennedy School;
Co-Founder of Cambridge Leadership Associates;
Co-Author, *Leadership on the Line* and
The Practice of Adaptive Leadership

INTRODUCTION

Imagine that the person you are secretly in love with gives you a present. "Here it is," they say with a smile on their face, as they hand you a large, oddly shaped box, carefully wrapped. You're surprised and about to open it when they remark: "But you have to wait three days to open it." "Three days?" you reply. What's in it, you wonder? The box feels heavy, but with its odd shape it could be anything. You shake it gently, but there is no sound or clue to its contents. Could it be the statement of love you've been yearning for, or perhaps something more mundane? You don't get much sleep that night. Your curiosity becomes insatiable and you feel you cannot wait another day – you want to know. Would you open the box before the three days were up?

When we want to know something, not knowing is tough. Most people's natural reaction to not knowing is to shun it. Yet to be human is not to know. We naturally turn to those who promise answers: the experts, the leaders and those who appear to know. We hold on to the knowledge we already have, we are afraid to let it go. We are neurologically hard-wired to avoid the unexpected and prefer certainty. Situations that are ambiguous or uncertain can make us feel incompetent, embarrassed and ashamed.

Yet we live in a world of uncertainty, complexity and volatility. We are unable to define the most complex challenges we face, let alone solve them. When we reach the edge of our knowledge, our default responses include clinging to our existing knowledge, attempting quick-fix solutions, or avoiding the situation altogether.

This book is about the problems that arise from our usual approach to the unknown, and it proposes a more fruitful relationship with not knowing. At the edge between the known and the unknown there is a fertile place, full of possibility. Playing at the edge can lead us to experience fresh new learning, creativity, joy and wonder. The edge is the place where something new can emerge. We call this Not Knowing. When we talk about Not Knowing (capitalized as a proper noun – "ing") we are suggesting a verb, a process, not a thing.

Books are traditionally vehicles for expertise and knowledge. As soon as we began work on this book, we were struck by the irony of writing about Not Knowing. How could we even imagine that we could write something knowledgeable about a topic that is, by its very nature, mysterious and unknown, even unknowable?

This book is not a "how-to" guide, and it does not provide easy answers either. Instead, it invites you to explore your own relationship with Not Knowing through the stories and experiences of others. The stories explore Not Knowing through a variety of lenses, such as art, science, literature, psychology, entrepreneurship, spirituality and the wisdom traditions. In researching this book we have curated a rich collection of diverse stories from all over the world. We meet people who have struggled with the unknown and, at the edge, discovered something that was not possible before, as well as people who are comfortable living and working at the edge.

A few of the stories are taken from history, but most are of recent or contemporary events, from people we have interviewed personally. We had the privilege of listening to their tales of Not Knowing, which were often shared with great honesty and vulnerability. With this in mind we have changed some names to respect anonymity. Although this book is primarily written for those in the world of work, we hope you can apply it to a range of situations in your personal and professional life. As authors, we have written this book with one collective voice, for clarity. Where we also share our own individual stories, we have highlighted this.

Our interest in writing about Not Knowing comes from our own experiences of being in the unknown. We both have a long history of fighting, resisting and, on many occasions, simply hating it.

Diana: I was born in Craiova, a town in the middle of rolling fields in the province of Oltenia in south-western Romania. My parents were respected artists – my father a stage and film actor and my mother a concert harpist. I remember a happy childhood overall, summers visiting the family farm and winters sledding down the hill near our house with my brother Stefan. Yet we lived with a constant uncertainty – that at any moment a neighbour could alert the secret police to a rebellious activity in thought or action.

With state-controlled media, it was common not to know about what was happening in the wider world. To fight the propaganda, my father would regularly listen to Radio Free Europe, which was broadcast from West Germany in defiance of communist censorship. Being caught listening to that crackly station meant interrogation by the secret police. The sounds of Radio Free Europe form a backdrop to my memories of childhood. I can still hear the main theme song in my head and the familiar murmur of voices.

I learned the day-to-day oppression of having knowledge denied and the power of knowing the truth.

I remember one balmy summer afternoon falling asleep at my grandmother's house in the countryside, and waking up to the news. The journalist was accusing former Romanian President Ceausescu of murdering children. It was the story the whole world found out about with horror after the Revolution in 1987. Chil-

dren were being kept like animals in orphanages without the basic necessities and adequate love and support.

I was only 12 years old and I still remember the shock of hearing that story. Not just the horrific details, but also the fact that I was now privy to secret knowledge that might place my family in danger.

In 1987 my father said "enough is enough" and we escaped Romania to Austria. That period in Austria was a time of utter Not Knowing – where we would live, what would happen to us, how it would all turn out. One year later we moved to Australia, where we were granted permanent residency as refugees. Another transition, another stage of Not Knowing - living in a new culture, learning a new language, starting a new school... From a childhood in a land of manipulated truth, to a time of uncertainty and change, I have lived and wrestled with Not Knowing.

Steven: In 2000 I was struggling to get out of bed and was losing weight, with a dry cough and pain in my lungs. As a stoical and stubborn man, I brushed off the symptoms until they became so painful that one morning I could not even tie my shoelaces. When I finally decided to go to the doctor, I was diagnosed with tuberculosis, which was drug-resistant and I was immediately sent to hospital. It meant an operation, many months of taking strong antibiotics and, at one point, as my condition was failing to respond I did not know if I was going to get well again.

I bought my first home in London at the height of the property market in 2006, just before the financial crash. Being cautious, I did a full survey before making the purchase and yet when I was just about to sell it I received a letter from the council saying that the render, windows, boundary fence and extension were all illegal. The previous owner had not acquired the necessary planning permissions and my solicitor had not picked this up. I was given a 30-day notice to remove the extension, which contained the only *toilet, kitchen and bathroom in the small cottage – so this would mean literally knocking down half the house. I appealed, but lived for over a year not knowing if I would have a home to come home to.*

At that time I worked in an investment bank - feeling secure and enjoying my job. One morning I got a call from a colleague saying that the name of our firm had changed. Overnight we had been bought out, to save the firm from financial collapse - a danger we knew nothing about, even the evening before. Projects were put on hold and every day we would see new emails wishing people well in their new endeavours as they were made redundant. After six months of constant uncertainty I was called into my manager's office with an HR representative and was made redundant in a phone call. Even though I was expecting it, it did not make it any easier and I was uncertain about what the future now held profes-sionally and how I was going to pay my mortgage.

In life choices I always seemed to be in a bind about making im-portant decisions. Should I take this option or should I take the other? When thinking about most decisions about the future and how to respond, I would paralyse myself, vacillating between op-tions that became constant dilemmas in my mind. A friend said to me, "Steven, you seem to embody hard decisions." It was painful and I hated the tyranny of choice and of not knowing what to do. I joked with them that I had a PhD in uncertainty! Life for me has been a constant struggle with Not Knowing, not only the more dramatic events I have described above, but the everyday choices I had to make. I only knew that there had to be a better way of being with the unknown."

Like you, we came to this book struggling with the unknown. The journey of researching and writing has helped us to develop a fresh relationship with Not Knowing. We are less eager to rely on our existing knowledge, more sceptical about those who pro-claim certainty, and more comfortable with being in a state of Not Knowing. We hope that you will experience this too.

At the end of the book we offer questions for reflection and experiments to play with to support you in developing your inquiry further.

As you commence your journey in this book, we invite you to bring along an exploratory mindset and to be open to the twists, turns and discoveries that you may make along the way. As the Spanish writer Antonio Machado said: *"Traveller, there is no path, the path is made by walking."*

PART I

Two kinds of intelligence

There are two kinds of intelligence: one acquired, as a child in school memorizes facts and concepts from books and from what the teacher says, collecting information from the traditional sciences as well as from the new sciences.

With such intelligence you rise in the world. You get ranked ahead or behind others in regard to your competence in retaining information. You stroll with this intelligence in and out of fields of knowledge, getting always more marks on your preserving tablets.

There is another kind of tablet, one already completed and preserved inside you. A spring overflowing its spring-box. A freshness in the center of the chest. This other intelligence does not turn yellow or stagnate. It's fluid, and it doesn't move from outside to inside through conduits of plumbing-learning.

This second knowing is a fountainhead from within you, moving out.

Rumi, Persian poet and Sufi mystic

CHAPTER 1

THE DANGERS   F KNOWLEDGE

O

1.

KNOWLEDGE IS POWERFUL

A child takes her first faltering steps and her parents grin with delight and gather her up in their arms for cuddles. She says her first words, performs a new song, or makes the final of the school spelling bee – and she gains praise and respect. From the very beginning, we are valued, appreciated and rewarded for accumulating knowledge and mastery.

Sir Francis Bacon's iconic phrase "knowledge is power" is so obvious that it doesn't bear mentioning. We know from school, work and life that expertise – being seen to know – determines our status and provides us with influence, power and reputation. The mere appearance of knowledge confers dignity and demands our attention.

In the past few decades, developed and developing economies have continued to shift inexorably towards services and away from agriculture and manufacturing. An increasing number of us are now in professions where we "think for a living." In many countries the attainment of a certain level of formal education increases average incomes through access to opportunities in employment. Higher levels of education are directly related to better health outcomes, lower fertility and longer lives.[1]

Beyond the practical benefits, the rank and power that we can draw from our knowledge and expertise can make us feel more important and more worthy. In turn this gives us more confidence. It may fuel our ambition as we seek to grow the status that comes with success.

Author and philosopher Nassim Nicholas Taleb tells us that we tend to treat our knowledge as *"personal property to be protected and defended. It is an ornament that allows us to rise in the pecking order. We take what we know quite seriously."*[2] Our thirst for knowledge is continuously fed by organizations that put a premium on competence and expertise. Performance according to specific criteria is evaluated and linked to promotions, remuneration, bonuses and other rewards. These reinforce the belief that the more competent we are, the more successful we will become, the higher up we will go, and the more we will get paid.

The rewards we acquire from knowledge, from certainty, are not only external – they are hard-wired into our brains. Recent studies in the field of neuroscience have shown that certainty is one of the key conditions we need to learn to function optimally. Neuroscientist David Rock even argues that threats to our certainty can be neurologically as painful as a physical attack.[3] This is supported by other research on the effect of uncertainty on the brain that shows that even a small amount of uncertainty generates an "error" response in the brain. It is debilitating to live with significant uncertainties, such as not knowing our boss's expectations or having to wait for medical results to find out if we have a serious illness. Our brain is always searching for the answer.

Neuroscientist Michael Gazzaniga, from the University of California, has researched this rationalization by studying those who have had hemispheres of their brains severed as a treatment for severe epilepsy. Applying the same experiment to each half separately, Gazzaniga was able to conclude that in the left hemisphere of the brain there is a neural network he calls "the Interpreter." The left hemisphere's capacity of continual interpretation means that it is *"always looking for order and reason, even when they don't exist."*[4]

It is little wonder we voraciously pursue knowledge in all its forms because knowledge is a wonderful thing. It promises that we will be rewarded, respected, promoted, and become wealthier, healthier and more confident.

Yet perhaps a little caution is in order. When was the last time someone tried to sell you something with many benefits, but no downsides? The problem with knowledge is in the very fact that it is so useful. We cling to it even in situations when it has the potential to limit us – to paradoxically get in the way of new learning and growth.

YOUR
KNOWLEDGE

● COMFORT ZONE

○ NOT KNOWING

NEW IDEAS
FREEDOM
CREATIVITY
FLUIDITY
SILENCE
EXCITEMENT
COURAGE
MINDFULNESS
OPP   TY
IN'   E
T   I
C   Y
Ь   J
A   E
LEARNING
LIGHT
AWARENESS
INFORMATION
REALIZATION
SPACE
IMMUNITY
FLEXIBILITY
INTELLIGENCE

2.

THE ALLURE OF THE KNOWN

Padua 1537. Andreas Vesalius, a young Flemish anatomist, enters the city gates heading for the university, with a few belongings and a burning desire to understand the human body. He'd arrived in the right place, at the right time. The Renaissance city of Padua, lying 35km west of Venice, was quickly becoming an international hot bed for the development of the arts and sciences. Vesalius joined what was considered at the time to be the most distinguished school of medicine and anatomy in Europe, founded more than 200 years earlier.[5]

Born in Brussels in 1514, the son of a court apothecary, as a child Vesalius became fascinated by the body. He was often found with dismembered dogs, cats and mice that he'd caught in the neighbourhood to dissect,[6] and would later steal a corpse from the gallows to obtain a complete human skeleton,[7] at great risk to himself and his family. At 18 his passion for learning about the body took him to Paris, where he commenced his medical studies. It was there that he first came across the seminal anatomy work of Galen of Pergamon, a Greek physician, surgeon and philosopher.

Galen was an influential figure in the world of medicine. His writings had been informed by his extensive experience treating the injuries of gladiators, serving as a physician to three Roman emperors. What had made his work so useful was that he had explained not just the structure of the human body, but the intricacies of the body's workings. For example, he demonstrated that the larynx generates the voice and was the first to recognize that there were distinct differences between venous (dark) and arterial (bright) blood. His work was slavishly followed by doctors over the centuries, who unequivocally believed in the accuracy of his claims. So although more than 1,400 years old, Galen's studies of the human body had remained the key references for anatomists and physicians and formed much of the basis for medical training in Europe during the Renaissance.

Like many students before him, Vesalius was fascinated by Galen's findings, which he initially found to be clear and persuasive. However, as he immersed himself in anatomical studies and read the Galenic texts more critically, Vesalius started noticing discrepancies and small mistakes. His doubts about some of Galen's claims were further reinforced by his experience attending many private and public lectures at the university.

In those days dissections were a grand affair, carried out before large audiences of students and invited guest scholars. These were highly ritualized and controlled events, bound in tradition and rigid rules set down by the university. A professor of anatomy would preside from a large, raised chair, removed from the actual proceedings. His only role was to read from Galen's anatomical texts while a surgeon would perform the actual dissection and a demonstrator would point out the specific parts of the body that were being examined. Even though these dissections were carried out by experienced scholars, it seemed to Vesalius that the work served to reinforce the old Galenic texts, rather than acting as an opportunity for new learning. This blind obedience to Galen was so strong that even when the surgeon held a human heart he would comment on three ventricles as outlined in Galen, in spite of him seeing that there were four. As Vesalius commented in a book a few years later, contradicting the authority of Galen was unthinkable, *"almost as if I were secretly to doubt the immortality of the soul."*[8]

Galen's book represented the state of knowledge, the known certainties, the place of comfort. And although Roman anatomy might seem quaint today, we still make similar errors in relying on the certainty of our existing knowledge.

3.

OVERCONFIDENCE BLINKERS

"Overconfident professionals sincerely believe they have expertise, act as experts and look like experts. You will have to struggle to remind yourself that they may be in the grip of an illusion."

Psychologist Daniel Kahneman

Maximilien de Robespierre, Galileo Lovano, Bonnie Prince Lorenzo, Wounded Knee, Queen Shaddock, Pygmalion, Murphy's Last Ride, Doctor Faustus. Do you recognize any of these?

These were the historical names and events that a team of researchers, led by Cameron Anderson from Haas School of Business, University of California, gave 243 MBA students at the beginning of the semester. The students had to identify which ones they knew or recognized. Mixed in with the real names, the researchers included made-up ones such as Galileo Lovano, Bonnie Prince Lorenzo, Queen Shaddock, and Murphy's Last Ride (you knew that, didn't you?). Those students who selected the most invented names were considered to be the most overly confident, because they believed they were more knowledgeable than they actually were.[9]

A survey at the end of the semester revealed that those same overly confident individuals achieved the highest social status within their groups. They engendered respect among their peers, tending to be more admired, listened to and generally having more influence in the group's decisions. Anderson noted that the group members did not think of their high-status peers as over-confident. They simply thought that they were fantastic, so their overconfidence did not come across as arrogant or narcissistic, but as a sign of their wonderful natures.[10]

A sense of realistic confidence, based on competence, is vital for surviving and thriving in the world. A lack of realistic confidence results in low esteem, under-performance in the workplace, poor relationships and can have negative consequences for our mental health and our quality of life.[11] Conversely, taking Anderson's research one step further, realistically confident people tend to attract success and achievement in their chosen fields, including getting the jobs they apply for, promotions, clinching the big deals, or winning the big accounts.[12]

Realistic confidence doesn't get us in trouble, but its bedfellow, overconfidence, does. Overconfidence is a bias where we inaccurately perceive and assess our judgement and abilities as being overly positive. Research carried out over more than 50 years shows that people have an overwhelming propensity to rate themselves as being "above average" in almost all respects. For example, motorcyclists believe that they are less likely to cause an accident than the typical motorcyclist, and business leaders believe their company is more likely to succeed than the average firm in their industry. Research also shows that 94% of university professors say that they do above-average work, surgical trainees place too much confidence in their diagnoses after looking at X-ray evidence, and clinical psychologists overestimate the chance that their predictions will prove accurate.[13] Despite its pitfalls, overconfidence is still common due to its profound social benefits. In the political arena, for example, it has been shown that if voters find confident politicians more credible, then contenders for leadership learn that to win an election, they need to express more confidence than their opponents.[14]

Professions that rely on the accumulation of knowledge and expertise must then be cautious about falling victim to their own overconfidence and the expectations of those who rely on them for advice. Heraclitus' words recorded more than 2,500 years ago still ring true today:

"Although we need the Word to keep things known in the common, people still treat specialists as if their nonsense were a form of wisdom."

Diagnosed with prostate cancer in 1995, Andy Grove, then CEO of Intel, was dismayed by the doctors' straightforward and categorical advice that surgery was the best treatment option for him. Nicknamed "Let's think for ourselves Grove" by his autobiographer Richard S Tedlow, Grove did not take the advice of doctors at face value. As someone who had survived both the Nazis and the communists before migrating from Hungary to the US in the 1950s, Grove was determined to explore the best options available to him to survive the cancer. He undertook extensive research into his illness, which quickly revealed alternatives to surgery. He uncovered data that was readily available, but which none of his doctors had mentioned or advised him to take seriously. Shocked to be confronted with the narrow mindset of his doctors, Grove settled on an alternative procedure known as "radiation seeding."

When Grove asked the doctor who carried out this procedure what he would do if he were in his shoes, the doctor said that he would probably have surgery. Then he continued to explain to a surprised Grove: *"You know, all through medical training, they drummed into us that the gold standard for prostate cancer is surgery. I guess that still shapes my thinking."*[15]

In an article he wrote for *Fortune* magazine in 1996, "Taking On Prostrate Cancer," Grove recalls the words of Dr Thomas A Stamey, the head of the urology department at Stanford University at the time, who explained the challenge facing the medical profession:

"...when faced with a serious illness beyond our comprehension [each of us] becomes childlike, afraid, and looking for someone to tell us what to do. It is an awesome responsibility for the surgeon to present the options to a patient with prostate cancer in such a way that he does not impose his prejudices, which may or may not be based on the best objective information. I think we have a long way to go to reach this ideal."

The reality is that the very thing that enables people to become experts and contribute to their own field, their deep knowledge and specific focus of research, may also limit their perspective. People who are recognized in their area of expertise and rewarded for their specialization usually don't have the incentive to look outside that area. The more specialized they become, the narrower their view may become. Experts are often too invested in what they know to question what they know, or to admit that they don't know.[16]

4.

THE LIMITS OF SPECIALIZATION

*"If you can't explain it simply,
you don't understand it well enough."*

Albert Einstein

In their constant search for competitive advantage, organizations are seeking people who already have specialized knowledge. This encourages people to keep going deeper rather than wider in their formal and informal learning. In our work we have observed the tendency for people to want to keep improving the skills they have already developed, rather than invest in gaining new ones. People are only too aware of the costs of training for years in one area, only to abandon it and "start from scratch" again.

Specialization has benefits, but it also comes with a risk: the more competent we are, the more we are prone to falling prey to "the curse of knowledge." The curse of knowledge means that the more you know, the harder it is to think and talk about your area of expertise in a simple way.[17] We tend to communicate from too high a level, misjudging other people's ability to understand us, causing confusion and hindering the learning of others. Where the task is to communicate knowledge, this curse can neuter the benefits of the knowledge as it fails to be received by the intended audience.

Complex or jargon-laden language can also mask genuine knowledge – where an amateur has learned the relevant buzzwords or jargon and uses them to create the impression of knowledge. The audience is left worse off, whether they are confused by a true specialist or misled by someone who does not possess expertise but who artfully uses jargon as a cover for their own ignorance.

Specialist knowledge can also impair fresh thinking about complex problems. As authors of *The Curse of Knowledge,* Chip and Dan Heath note: *"When we are given knowledge, it is impossible to imagine what it's like to LACK that knowledge."*[18] The more expertise we have on a particular topic, the harder it is for us to frame the problem in a neutral way that everyone will understand. Inbuilt in our definition of the problem is our own perspective of it. Our knowledge and expertise limit our perspective and the exploration of possible solutions, and make it difficult for us to think laterally or "outside the box." Behavioural economists call this "anchoring bias" – where the nature of the problem is already well established, or "anchored" by existing knowledge.[19]

The International AIDS Vaccine Initiative is a research prize set up to help find fresh solutions to combating HIV. The Initiative sponsored an open challenge to the scientific community to come up with an effective inoculation for the virus. Unfortunately, defining the Request for Proposal as a vaccine challenge did not yield many high-quality responses. This was because the specialists had inadvertently "anchored" the problem to vaccines, so the thinking was inevitably limited to finding solutions that happen to be vaccines. In a way, this is a form of prejudice – the solution is prejudged as being a vaccine, when non-vaccine solutions may be superior. As the saying goes: *"If you are a hammer, then everything looks like a nail."*

An innovation consultant, Andy Zynga, suggested framing the problem as a protein stabilization challenge, rather than a vaccine development challenge.[20] By reframing the challenge around the problem (protein stabilization) rather than the type of solution (vaccine), the challenge was opened up to a wider range of thinkers and experts. With this reframing, 34 proposals were received from highly qualified scientists in 14 countries, covering wider and more innovative thinking than previous solutions. Three of these were selected to receive research grants. If organizations or people have high levels of expertise, sometimes the boundaries of their expertise limit their ability to think about a problem from fresh angles.

In his book *Expert Political Judgement*[21] Philip Tetlock, Professor of Psychology and Management at the University of Pennsylvania, analyzed more than 2,500 forecasts by experts and then what actually happened. An analogy from the writing of the Greek poet Archilochus divides people into two categories: 'foxes' and 'hedgehogs'. The fox knows many things, but the expert hedgehog knows one big thing. Tetlock discovered that the foxes were generally more accurate in their predictions than the expert hedgehogs. Part of the reason for this was that the narrow focus of the expert prevented them from seeing the bigger picture of factors beyond their specialization. So according to Tetlock, knowing a lot can make someone less reliable in being able to make forecasts. He also found that often there was an overconfidence that made experts blind to contradictory opinions: a case of hubris. *"Experts in demand were more overconfident than their colleagues who eked out existences far from the limelight,"* says Tetlock.[22]

5.

WILFUL BLINDNESS

*"Many fail to grasp what they have seen,
and cannot judge what they have learned,
although they tell themselves
they know."*

Heraclitus

Libby is a charming town in a northwest corner of Montana, near the border with Canada. The community of 2,600 sits in the narrow Kootenai River valley carved by glaciers and surrounded by forested mountains. If you passed through Libby your first impressions would be of quaint cafes, old-world shops and "I love Libby" signs at every corner. It is a typical US country town, but there is nothing typical about Libby. Among the breath-taking scenery and quiet streets, a tragedy has been slowly unfolding.

For more than 50 years, the community of Libby has been battling with an epidemic of asbestosis and asbestos-related diseases, which has killed hundreds of people and has affected three generations of families in the town. The mortality rate for Libby is 80 times higher than for the rest of the US, and new cases are continuing to be diagnosed all the time. The Environmental Protection Authority (EPA) has called this "the most horrific environmental disaster in US history" and Libby has become known as "ground zero."

Knowledge to
become an **EXPER**

S E can limit and
arrow your perspective

The disaster is linked to a vermiculite mine near Libby that was acquired by the WR Grace Company in 1963. The problem is not vermiculite itself, but the fact that it is found in rocks laced with tremolite, the most toxic form of asbestos. Under a microscope, the long tremolite fibres appear as barbed hooks, which when inhaled, grab onto the lung tissue and wreak havoc.

By the early 1960s it was known that asbestos caused lung disease. An internal company memo, written in 1955, referred to *"the dangers of exposing our employees to asbestos"* and many employees' chest X-rays were showing early signs of asbestosis, though the affected people were never informed.

The residents of Libby have also been exposed to the toxic dust. *"It was everywhere. It was so fine you couldn't see it in the air, but you could see it settling in your coffee,"* said former miner, Bob Wilkins, in a radio interview. People in the community started to become ill and die from asbestosis in the early 1960s. By 1990 one in four families was being affected by respiratory illnesses and there was a funeral almost every week. In spite of mounting evidence that there was something terribly wrong going on in this community, the local, state and federal authorities did nothing about it. They and the community turned a blind eye for more than 30 years and the mining company responsible rejected the idea that they had anything to do with the illnesses and deaths.

Then a local woman named Gayla Benefield spoke up. Described as *"a bit older than Erin Brockovich, but with the same smart mouth,"*[23] Benefield has become an icon for the fight to raise awareness of this tragedy, and to bring those responsible to justice. Over the past 40 years, more than 30 members of Benefield's family have died from lung-related illnesses, including both her parents and others close to her are affected by it, including her daughter and her granddaughter.

You would think that such a large-scale disaster, with such tragic consequences, would be hard to ignore. But this is what the town's residents did, in spite of overwhelming evidence and direct, personal contact with the epidemic. Most lost friends, neighbours and family, but they went about their daily lives as if nothing was wrong. Libby was a town in mourning, a community gasping for air, literally, but nobody was prepared to admit it; Libby is a classic case of wilful blindness.

When Benefield tried to talk to people about what seemed obvious to her, she received a variety of reactions. They ignored, avoided, ridiculed, marginalized, resisted and denied what she said. It was those residents whose health was unaffected that were most sceptical about the health consequences for others. They argued that if the situation had been that dangerous, then surely someone would have done something about it. The doctors would have spoken out or the authorities would have intervened. What would Benefield, a middle-aged local, know about asbestosis anyway? Many insisted that Libby was fine; they thought it to be a perfectly safe place to live and raise a family – *"everybody knows there's nothing wrong with this town."*[24] Some people even made a bumper sticker, which said: *"I am from Libby Montana and I don't have asbestosis."*

The community became split between those who believed in Benefield's claims and those who didn't even want to talk about it. In spite of general perceptions of Libby being a caring and supportive community, sufferers of the disease were given the cold shoulder at best, and met with anger and resentment at worst. It was as though the whole world had conspired to ignore the plain truth. Even the EPA initially met the news with skepticism. Like everyone else before him, Paul Peronard's (the EPA team leader called to investigate the Libby situation) initial reaction was *"If something this bad had happened, we'd know about it. Hell, everybody would know about it. It's got to be bullshit."*[25]

But Benefield did not give up. Eventually cleanup teams wearing protective clothing started appearing in the town, cordoning off toxic sites with tapes, lifting tons of contaminated soil and trucking it away, moving whole families out of their homes and covering the houses in plastic. But even then some townsfolk refused to accept the reality of the situation. When an asbestosis clinic opened in Libby, people initially went in through the back door, hating to admit that Benefield had been right all along.[26]

The mining company, WR Grace, continued to deny that there was a problem until it was proven otherwise in court. The company was ordered to pay compensation to the families affected by the disease. Slowly people started to come to terms with the enormity of their town's tragedy. The bumper stickers changed and now read *"We're doing asbestos we can."*

What would have happened if the townsfolk, the authorities and the politicians, when they first heard of the possibility of asbestosis, had said "I don't know what's going on?" What would have happened if they had opened the issue up to investigation? Their reliance on what they already "knew," that Libby was a safe place to raise kids and a wonderful community, was unshakeable. Their holding on to what they knew left no space for doubt, for Not Knowing, and this had led to disastrous consequences.

6.
THE PRETENCE OF KNOWLEDGE

*"It's not a good idea to take a forecast
from someone wearing a tie."*

Nassim Nicholas Taleb

When Friedrich Hayek won the Nobel Prize for economics in 1974, he entitled his winner's speech "The Pretense of Knowledge" and warned against making policy based on the omniscience assumed in classical economic theory. Since then research has consistently shown that there are problems attached to relying on experts' predictions – because they are often wrong.[27]

In November 2008, at the height of the financial crisis, after the collapse of the investment bank Lehman Brothers, Queen Elizabeth II visited the London School of Economics. She asked the crowd of distinguished economists a simple yet devastating question: *"Why had nobody noticed that the credit crunch was on its way?"*

On 17 June 2009 the British Academy convened a forum with experts, academics and representatives from the City of London, business, regulators and government to debate the answer.

The letter, which was released after an embargo on 26 July 2009, pointed out that for many the crisis was not an unknown. In fact, it was predictable. *"Many people did foresee the crisis... There were many warnings about imbalances in financial markets and in the global economy. For example, the Bank of International Settlements expressed repeated concerns that risks did not seem to be properly reflected in financial markets."* It goes on to say that the Bank of England issued many warnings in their bi-annual Financial Stability Reports. There certainly was no shortage of risk managers – one bank reputedly had 4,000 of them.

In fact, it was not an issue of not being given a warning. The letter identifies the problem as an overconfidence in the expertise of the few; the belief that they knew what they were doing and a blind trust in expertise in a complex situation.

"But against those who warned, most were convinced that banks knew what they were doing. They believed that the financial wizards had found new and clever ways of managing risks. Indeed, some claimed to have so dispersed them through an array of novel financial instruments that they had virtually removed them. It is difficult to recall a greater example of wishful thinking combined with hubris... Nobody wanted to believe that their judgement could be faulty or that they were unable competently to scrutinize the risks in the organizations that they managed. A generation of bankers and financiers deceived themselves and those who thought they were the pace-making engineers of advanced economies."[28]

The signatories acknowledge that the climate of light-touch regulation, low interest rates and inflation also contributed to the situation. The letter makes it clear, however, that although each individual that played a role was perfectly intelligent, this was a collective failure in which hubris, herd psychology and blind faith in experts played a key role.

Around the same time, Alan Greenspan, the then Chairman of the Federal Reserve of the US, acknowledged the challenge of predicting the global financial crisis: *"The Federal Reserve was as good an economic organization as exists,"* Greenspan said. *"If all those extraordinarily capable people were unable to foresee the development of this critical problem . . . we have to ask ourselves: Why is that? And the answer is that we're not smart enough as people. We just cannot see events that far in advance."*[29]

Even though we might not want to admit it, human beings have severe cognitive limits. Take chess. Most people would agree that a grand master of chess (as of 2013 there are only 1,441 in the world[30]) has extraordinary cognitive abilities, especially in chess. Yet a grand master can only think 10-15 moves ahead in chess, a game with fixed and consistent rules. Compare a game of chess with that of the world economy. It is folly to imagine that any person, or even 4,000 risk managers, could possibly see ahead to accurately predict the movements in markets – markets where millions of individual actors make millions of intersecting choices that are both rational and irrational, predictable and chaotic.

Gerd Gigerenzer, Director of the Centre for Adaptive Behaviour and Cognition at the Max Planck Institute in Berlin, marvels at the way people still blindly trust their financial advisors, clinging to the belief that other people can predict the future for them. Once a year, financial institutions conduct their annual forecast of the movements of the Dow and US dollar exchange rates, yet, as he reminds us: *"their track record is hardly better than chance. We pay $200 billion yearly to a forecasting industry that delivers mostly erroneous future predictions."*[31]

The experts were not the ones who understood and predicted the global financial crisis of 2008. As Tetlock (the fox and the hedgehog concept, page 44) shows, experts are normally the worst at making accurate predictions – the world moves faster than they are willing to acknowledge. When experts are challenged, they rarely admit that they are wrong, instead blaming changing circumstances.[32]

We acutely feel the pressure from those around us to mask our incompetence and inadequacy, to pretend that we have the answers, even when we don't – or we need to believe that someone else does. We look to the experts and assume that they know what they are doing. Sometimes even when the evidence is to the contrary, we would rather believe in someone else's false certainty than question it and use our own judgement. Nowhere is this dependency more acute than in our relationship with leaders.

DEPENDENCY ON EXPERTS
AND LEADERS

"beware
the shadow that
our knowledge
casts."

Process-Oriented Psychologist & Consultant Julie Diamond

1.

THE LEADER WHO KNEW TOO MUCH

Anna Simioni, the former Chief Learning Officer of a European financial institution, didn't care for studying and hated homework in primary school. She was an attentive student and did well, but would often trade homework with her classmates. She did not suffer from the view that she needed to "know"; she was happy with being "good enough."

At high school Anna started her own philosophical movement with a small group of friends, who called themselves *"Uncertaintists: The people who are not certain."* Their motto was *"never be absolute,"* because they believed that you could never really know for sure whether you were going or not going to do something that at a certain moment you believe or do not believe. When she went to university Anna was surprised to find that there was little room there for uncertainty. Her professors believed that there was a right and a wrong answer to questions and nothing in between. When she was tested with multiple-choice questions, she always thought that there were at least two possible correct answers, not just one, at least in some cases. Yet, her professors seemed to have no interest in engaging with her thinking. They would say *"this is the right answer; the other is wrong."*

Everything changed when Anna began a career in consultancy. As she says: *"I think that experience ruined me. I felt I needed to know the right answer for my clients. What drove me to know and increase my expertise was that I was a young woman, attractive and in a predominately male industry. I had a desperate desire to be valued for my competence. I did not want people to say 'she is here because she is pretty or nice'."* So with her family background, her university and her own expectations of her role,

Anna became embedded in a "right or wrong" way of thinking and competence became her key focus.

Anna quickly became considered a "top talent" in her organization. When she was 24, after a psychological assessment, an occupational psychologist told her that she had never seen a profile like hers: she had CEO potential. Anna was flattered and this reinforced her attachment to competence – her drive for competence and her increasing expertise had now been rewarded. She was promoted and won many "best performer" awards. However, her colleagues found her to be rigid in her approach and would call her "the protector of the method." While they were looking for ways to adapt the methodology to suit their clients' needs, Anna fought to preserve the approach rather than deviating from it.

By her 30s Anna had built a career on her own expertise and felt more self-confident and entitled to do what she wanted. *"At that time I was a difficult friend. My self-confidence and my attachment to my own point of view got in the way of my relationships. I had a very select group of friends and an incredibly close relationship with my core team. They loved my passion and stubbornness, but everybody else outside my core team suffered. I was too smart, too competent and perceived to be distant."*

Anna got a wake-up call when she did a 360-degree feedback exercise on her role. Her staff rated her 100% competent, but they reported that they did not enjoy working with her. They felt that they had no room to grow, make mistakes or contribute. They believed that their opinion did not matter, since she was always so competent and was always in control, excelling at everything she did. The impact on Anna's team was clear – they were not motivated to work for her. *"My team was, in some way, suffering from my 'know it all approach'."* When she first read the feedback report, Anna was very upset. *"I had great pride in being competent. In fact, I thought it was one of the best things that a manager could be. 'I would have loved to have a boss like me who was competent and fair!', I thought. In my view, I was doing the right thing. I was imparting confidence in the staff by telling them that 'this is the way we need to do things'."*

Anna can now see that her way of relating to her staff caused them to experience anxiety.

"If your manager knows everything and you don't, it is understandable that you might feel that you will never make it. If you have a manager like that and you feel 'ah this is difficult', or 'this is new and strange in our organization', then the knowledge of the manager can be disempowering. I wanted to introduce major change because it was needed, but I was hindering the change with my own behaviours."

Anna's knowledge and expertise were too distant from the reality of her staff's experience; she was telling them what they needed to do in a way that made them feel less, rather than more, capable. She has since learned that talking with people when they are anxious distorts the flow of communication. *"When there is something complex and difficult to be dealt with we tend to treat people like children: 'you know what, don't bother, I'll tell you how to do it'. We think this is helpful to them. I was really doing this in good faith, thinking that it was useful."*

However, all this time Anna was feeling awkward herself. The only way for her to deal with the anxiety of Not Knowing was to take an "I need to tell you" approach. Her assumption was that this would make people feel secure and help them to be more productive. She explains the pressure she felt in her role to know: *"I felt that I was the only one responsible for the results. I wanted to achieve good results; I wanted to do our best. There was a big challenge and the stakes were high. My belief that I was the one carrying the whole thing led me to think that I had to clearly tell my colleagues what to do. I knew what was needed and so it was a matter of 'follow me'. When this did not yield good outcomes in terms of negative tension, I became disappointed and could not understand why my staff were not motivated to operate the way I thought was the best."*

There are situations when we can know "too much" and this hinders progress. The expectation that the person in charge knows "everything," as in Anna's case, can have a debilitating impact on the people around us; it can be anxiety-provoking and disempowering. We limit our learning and growth through a tendency to over-rely on our knowledge and expertise. If we also manage staff, this can be to the detriment of the team since knowledge can end up having a perverse effect, a corrupting influence.

The pressures and demands placed on us by our workplaces contribute to the *illusion of knowledge*. They increase the propensity for us to become immune to doubts, contributing to many of us having to master the art of sounding as though we know what we are talking about, even if we have no idea. Surrounded by people who seek our approval and depend on us for our expertise, we fall prey to the illusion that we know what we are doing.

2.

THE PROBLEM WITH "CERTAIN" LEADERS

"Dogmatism and skepticism are both, in a sense, absolute philosophies; one is certain of knowing, the other of not knowing. What philosophy should dissipate is certainty, whether of knowledge or ignorance."

Philosopher Bertrand Russell

Do you remember where you were when you heard the news of Princess Diana's death or John F Kennedy's assassination? Or what you were doing when the planes struck the World Trade Center in New York? These tragedies are likely to be imprinted in our memories for ever. But how consistent and accurate are those memories over time? And how certain can we be?

Diana: I was working for an American Law firm in London and had just phoned a colleague in the Chicago office. I was trying to finish a report due the following morning, and I'd realized I was missing some really important figures. Within a few seconds of hearing my colleague's voice, I knew something was terribly wrong. "Sorry, I can't speak right now," he said in a panicked voice. "Our office in New York has been attacked. Turn on the TV," and he put down the phone. Puzzled, I left my office and went into the corridor, looking for someone to talk to. Most people were working calmly at their desks, when all of a sudden the Managing Partner came rushing past my office shouting

"We've been attacked!" Mayhem ensued. People followed him into the boardroom where pictures of a smoking tower were showing on the TV. We knew that the firm's New York office was on floors 54-59 of the North Tower of the World Trade Center. The room quickly filled with people huddled around, some crying, some staring at the screen in shock. Like most people who have witnessed or heard the news of traumatic events, I have vivid memories of that afternoon. I remember biting my nails hard and feeling torn between watching the screen and running out the door. I can describe in detail what I was wearing, who said what, and my surroundings. But research shows my memories of that day are not reliable.

These are known as "flashbulb memories," a term introduced in 1977 by psychologists Roger Brown and James Kulik. Their argument was that these highly dramatic events are so emotionally important to us that they're imprinted in our memories like a photograph, capturing all details vividly and accurately. Whenever the recollection of an event is accompanied by the words "I remember it as if it was yesterday" it is most likely pointing to a flashbulb memory in our lives.

What is interesting, though, is not just the research on the reliability of our memories (showing that the more time passes, the more memories deteriorate), but our high level of certainty about their accuracy. A study carried out by psychologist Ulric Neisser after the Challenger space shuttle explosion in January 1986 compared students' recollections immediately after the event with their recollections two and a half years later. The study revealed that 25% of the students gave a significantly different account of the event at the later date. What was even more startling, though, was when he showed those students their conflicting accounts of the events, pointing to the original handwritten notes, they vehemently expressed that they were absolutely certain that their false recollections were correct. One student even commented: *"That's my handwriting, but that's not what happened."*[33]

Experts are not immune from the certainty bias because the more committed we are to a belief, the harder it is to let go of it, or acknowledge that we are wrong.[34] It's as though we have an internal immune system that automatically attacks any invasion of doubt and ambiguity that we may encounter, or any challenge to our confirmed world view.

A knowledge based society places a high value on certainty and looking as though we know what we are talking about, being sure of ourselves, being on top of our subject matter, speaking with conviction; these all lead to us being seen as competent. Our need for certainty, to know what's going on, to work things out so that we can be useful is so ingrained that we might not even be aware of when it exerts pressure in our lives, how that manifests, and what the impact is. Our doubts are alleviated when someone looks as though they know what they are doing. Confidence breeds certainty, while doubt breeds uncertainty and a lack of trust in the capacity for the job. The illusion or fantasy that experts know what they are doing is immensely comforting.

In the first presidential debate between US President George W Bush and Senator John Kerry on 30 September 2004, Bush accused Kerry of changing positions on the war in Iraq.

"I just know how this world works, and that in the councils of government, there must be certainty from the US president. We change tactics when we need to, but we never change our beliefs, the strategic beliefs that are necessary to protect this country in the world."[35]

In response to that, Kerry argued that "certainty" can get you into trouble and that it would be better to acknowledge the facts and adapt the policy accordingly.[36] Bush won office, and his need to deliver certainty and conviction that he was right was one of the factors that led him to declare war in the Middle East – on the assumption that there were weapons of mass destruction there.

ARE
YOU
AWARE
OF
THE
SHADOW
YOUR
KNOWLEDGE
CASTS
ON
PEOPLE
AROUND
YOU?

Politicians don't have much room to manoeuvre. After running for a seat for the Labor Party in the Australian Federal Parliament on 7 September 2013, Nicole Lessio, a young politician from Brisbane, became convinced that the pressure to "know" is one of the primary barriers to increased political participation.

"The pressure is immense. You don't want to be the candidate to go viral in the media! You don't want to embarrass yourself and your family and you certainly don't want to embarrass your Party.

"There are huge risks in assuming or pretending knowledge, and the media (in particular) are very keen to capitalize on any error of fact. I did many interviews and all journalists were keen to 'catch me out' on facts and figures."

As an incumbent Member of Parliament, Nicole's opponent spends his whole working life focused on staying fully appraised of details. As the "amateur" challenger, she has the short "daily briefing" email on the events of the day from her Party Headquarters to fall back on. But mostly she has to rely entirely on her own general knowledge, specific knowledge in policy areas she is familiar with, and the uncomfortable unknown. *"It is an interesting paradox – the media and the public expect you to be a 'regular' person (i.e. not a politician, because they detest the professionalization of politics) but at the same time expect you to know every minute detail of each policy platform. It is challenging to traverse."*

In answer to questions put to her during a public forum, Nicole responded with *"that isn't something I'm completely sure of. Can I get your details, take that question on notice and get back to you?"* She reflects that other candidates on the panel seemed to feel greater pressure to know and so pretended knowledge on a variety of issues. *"Some voters quite happily lapped up the incorrect information they were fed, while others scoffed at the obvious errors. I can only suspect that had I made such errors, they would have found their way onto the news as a number of voters filmed proceedings,"* says Nicole.

The expectations laid on politicians are like straitjackets, making it hard for them to change their minds. Margaret Thatcher, former UK Prime Minister, famously declared that "the lady's not for turning" and refused to display any signs of weakness. When the former Australian Prime Minister, Kevin Rudd, changed his position on marriage equality in a blog post on his website on 20 May 2013, Nicole celebrated. She posted it on her campaign Facebook page and was deluged with messages – most were supportive but some were appalled that Rudd had changed his mind.

Nicole's story illustrates the impossible double bind that many of us face. How can we hold doubt and be truthful about the limits of our knowledge on the one hand, whilst meeting other people's expectations to be certain on the other?

3.

THE WEIGHT OF EXPECTATIONS

Research carried out by Yiannis Gabriel, Professor of Organizational Theory at the University of Bath, shows that the expectations laid on people in charge to be all-knowing and all-powerful are shaped by our own childhood experiences. Parenting is the first all-knowing, all-powerful role that we experience in our lives and our parents, or those who raise us, start by being the centre of the universe for us. We are born completely powerless and dependent on them to provide us with food, shelter and love. If we are lucky, they are there when we take our first steps, picking us up when we stumble, orienting us to the world around us, shedding light on puzzling ideas or situations, and comforting us in times of trouble. Parents are the experts on everything in their children's eyes.

In spite of vivid memories of our parents' failings and mistakes, many of us still carry this illusion of perfection and omnipotence into the workplace. It affects our relationships with bosses and underlines the expectations we have of people in charge. We have an ingrained need for authority figures. We want to believe that there is someone out there who can solve the problems we are facing, to help us, to "save" us, even though our experience tells us otherwise, and we may have been disappointed many times before.

This is illustrated in the way Caroline, a project manager in the IT department of a large company, describes her relationship with her manager.

"Jane is someone I can go to for advice. She always makes time for me, for which I am really grateful. When I first started in the department she took me under her wing and we would spend some lunchtimes together, talking about the business. I had so much

to learn and the stakes were very high. We were in the process of rolling out a fresh technology platform and everyone was stressed. I knew that Jane had it all under control and her confidence was reassuring. Just like watching the flight attendants during a bumpy ride, all eyes were on her to see how she would react. At one point we dropped the ball and had some setbacks. Under Jane's direction we were able to regroup and refocus. It was a challenging time, but the team worked really well together. Jane is able to solve any problem that you bring to her. There's nothing that she can't do. I have so much to learn from her!"

The higher the uncertainty we find ourselves in, the higher our propensity to depend on the people in charge to provide clarity, to assure us that we will be OK.

> ***Steven:*** *I was working with the management team of a large media organization. All the leaders were smart, co-operative and had known each other well for a number of years. As an icebreaker to explore behaviour under uncertainty, together with a colleague, I asked them to play a game called "traffic jam." This involved two teams facing each other, with an empty space in between. Each person could take one step forward, but only into an empty space. The object of the game was for the two teams to exchange places. As the game started, the teams had fun experimenting with possibilities. First they began to look for someone who could guide the team through based on prior experience. "Has anyone played this before or something similar?" was asked. As the time pressure increased, individuals broke away and attempted to solve the problem on paper, while the rest of the team waited by in frustration. Near the end of the session the senior leaders became exasperated, becoming more autocratic, issuing commands and telling people what to do. Towards the end the task was still not complete so the team started looking for someone to help save them from failing to complete the task. "Can you help us?" they asked one of the facilitators in desperation. It is easy to collaborate when the pressure is low. Under stress, however, the team became dependent on the people in charge to solve the problem they were facing.*

We follow people because of what they know, not because of what they don't know. We engage consultants because they know something that we don't.

The pressure is not just to be competent but also to take decisive action. Can Caroline, the IT project manager above, solve all of her team's problems? It's unlikely. Does she always know what to do? Again, this is highly unlikely. As another senior manager said to us, *"I kind of feel obliged in being a leader and a professional to have the answers. I feel the expectation from others that I have to 'know'. That is what I am there for."* Under the weight of these expectations, we may be forgiven for feeling compelled to provide short-term fixes. These may temporarily alleviate the tension and the uncertainty, but in the long run they may get in the way of making any real progress on the challenges.

Sometimes these high expectations can even lead to us being dishonest with ourselves and with others.

4.

PRETENDING TO KNOW

Pretending to know is common, no matter what our role or level. This is because it feels as though faking knowledge or knowing is better than disappointing people: it's better than looking incompetent or losing people's trust, as Nash Kay[37] found out when he was a junior sales executive on rotation in the commercial department of a television studio in Lebanon. He had yet to prove himself and had a poor relationship with his manager.

At 60, Peter, Nash's boss, had taken the department to a whole new level by regularly securing multimillion deals, acquiring more credibility and power along the way. His was a brash character: while he was extremely secretive and ensured everyone was kept on a need-to-know basis, he also despised incompetence and people who did not have answers. Yet he, himself, rarely gave any answers.

One day, Peter stormed into Nash's office: *"I need a competent person now – someone with stellar analytical skills, sharp business acumen and the mindset of a consultant. Do you have that?"*

Nash's heart was pounding and his right eye started to twitch. He had none of the requirements Peter had listed: he didn't have analytical skills or any experience in consulting.

"Did you hear what I said?" repeated Peter. Nash tried to remain as composed as possible and against his better judgement said *"Yes, I have all that."*
Peter promptly responded: *"Great. We meet at 2pm in the conference room"* and ran out of the room.

"It is true; I lied," reflects Nash. *"Not only that, I had also implicated myself in something I had no information about, undermined my own manager and potentially compromised my department. Why? Was I intimidated by the presence of such an impressive character and senior manager? Was I attempting to preserve my job? After all, I felt that rejecting the request of someone like Peter was nothing less than professional suicide, especially in our business. Or was I gambling by attempting to grasp onto what I perceived to be an exciting venture that could move me up the ladder faster? Perhaps it was a little of everything."*

As a consequence of lying to Peter about his abilities Nash was in turmoil. For weeks he worked like a slave, reading up on finance, break-even analysis and a range of business concepts that were new to him. He tried to keep up in the meetings, but so much was a mystery to him. He was sure Peter was looking at him disapprovingly. On top of this, he was sleeping for only three hours a night and came to feel that he wanted to resign – just to avoid the pressure. However, three months later he had managed to prove himself and deliver the high performance expected of him, but at a considerable cost to his own physical and mental health.

When we are faced with a dilemma, a difficult problem to solve, or a new situation we've never encountered before, we generally believe that we have limited options and tend to paper over the gaps in our knowledge. We either pretend to the world that we have the knowledge and expertise, or we cling to our existing knowledge. Although pretending to know can stretch us into new territory, as in Nash's case, it is just as likely to get us into trouble when the gaps become obvious.

5.
BLIND OBEDIENCE TO AUTHORITY

*"Do not believe in anything merely on the
authority of your teachers and elders.
Do not believe in traditions just because
they have been handed down
for many generations."*

Buddha

The 2011 crash of a Polish airplane at Smolensk in Russia was
a national tragedy and a time of mourning was declared in both
countries. The exact causes of the crash and who or what was
to blame are disputed to this day. A range of causes was considered, from poor lighting, incorrect information by Russian
air traffic control, pilot error, trees not being cut near the run-
way, to the actual location of the landing being incorrect.

The Russian report on the crash provides an intriguing perspective on the accident. It argued that the Polish crew failed to heed
bad weather warnings because they were afraid of displeasing
their President, Lech Kaczynski. Tatayana Anodina, head of the
Interstate Aviation Committee (MAK) in Moscow, who inves-
tigated the accident, argued that the pilots were driven to take
"unjustified risks."[38] She said that during the flight, the crew
was repeatedly advised of bad weather conditions at the destination airport, but despite this failed to change course in order
to make an alternative landing. Her view was that the two pilots

had feared a "negative reaction" from President Kaczynski if they switched to the other airfield.

"The main passenger's expected negative reaction... placed psychological pressure on crew members and influenced the decision to continue the landing," she said. The plane's flight recorder caught one of the crew saying *"He'll get mad,"* in an apparent reference to the Polish President's determination not to alter his schedule. Poland's air force commander, Gen Andrzej Blasik, added to the pressure by entering the flight deck, Anodina noted:

"The presence of the Polish air force commander on the flight deck up to the aircraft's impact with the ground put psychological pressure on the crew captain to decide on continuing descent in a situation of unjustified risk, dominated by the goal of making a landing at any cost."

Whether the Russian version of the cause of the accident is correct or not, the story illustrates the dangers associated with the pressure to comply with people in authority. This pressure can be exercised even when the authority figure is not known personally or is not even present.

In the 2012 American docudrama *Compliance* a young woman was humiliated by her manager, and sexually assaulted by a stranger, who was receiving instructions over the phone from a man who falsely identified himself as a police officer. The film directors claimed that this incident was not isolated, but had happened more than 80 times in different states in the US. The film depicts the helplessness and anguish of the victim and also the moral dilemma of the perpetrator who was seeking to do the right thing within their paradigm in relationship to the authority figure. Why is it that the authority figure was not even questioned and degrading acts were committed, all in the name of following the "law?"

When we have a compliant relationship with authority it relieves the anxiety and pain of Not Knowing. However, blind obedience may significantly impact on people's ability to make good decisions and perform at their peak. At worst, it can lead to devastating consequences.

THE SOLID FOUNDATION

OF WHAT YOU KNOW

GROWTH OF THE UNKNOWN

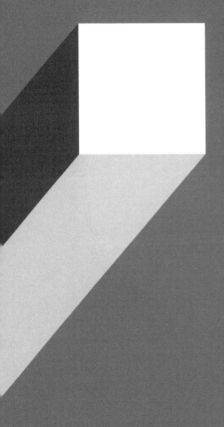

CHAPTER 3

"KNOWLEDGE IS LIKE A SPHERE. THE GREATER ITS VOLUME, THE LARGER ITS CONTACT WITH THE UNKNOWN"

17th-century mathematician, Blaise Pascal

1.

KNOWLEDGE KEEPS CHANGING

Despite the speed of change in the world generally, we often rely on our existing knowledge to understand it, even when that may not be useful or accurate. Perceptions or facts about the world may be static in our minds, even though they are changing dramatically all the time.

In May 2013 Swedish professor Hans Rosling asked 1,000 British people to take a test on population growth. The questions were deceptively straightforward, such as:

How many children do UN experts estimate there will be by the year 2100? What percentage of adults in the world today are literate – i.e. can read and write? What is the life expectancy in the world as a whole today?

If you did the questionnaire, you might be surprised to find that you knew less about the world than chimpanzees. As Rosling explains: *"If for each question I wrote each of the possible alternatives on bananas, and asked chimpanzees in the zoo to pick the right answers, by picking the right bananas, they'd just pick bananas at random."*[43]

A striking fact in Rosling's findings is that the pollsters with university education did not do any better, and sometimes even worse, than the general population, including some of his university professor colleagues. Rosling's research provides a reality check about the world, and shows how most people are ignorant about the ways the world is changing for the better. His research also reveals how we rely on preconceived ideas that are years, or sometimes decades, out of date. As the world is changing so rapidly, we increasingly find ourselves in situations where what we know, or what we thought we knew, is no longer useful or correct.

Take the rapid progress of knowledge itself. If we think about anatomy at the time of Vesalius, whose story appears earlier (see page 34), how could a book about how the body worked survive 1,400 years as being the gospel truth?

American scientist Ray Kurzweil argues that at the current rate of scientific progress, we'll make the same amount of progress as occurred in the 20th century in 14 years, and then again in seven years. This is 1,000 times faster progress than the progress achieved in the 20th century. He also predicts that in 15 years' time the internet will contain all accessible human knowledge.[44] Knowledge seems to be expanding at an accelerating pace.

You would think that the more that knowledge expands, the more we know, and by definition, the less we don't know. The problem with this thinking is that it assumes that the total universe of knowable things is fixed.

2.

MORE COMPLEX, MORE AMBIGUOUS

The challenges we face today in the workplace and in the world are becoming increasingly complex. We are confronted with ambiguous problems that can't be described, let alone carried out and solved. The world has become more volatile, more uncertain, more complex and more ambiguous. This is commonly described by the acronym VUCA: Volatile, Uncertain, Complex and Ambiguous. These concepts are not new but they magnify the dangers of relying on what we know.

In April 2013 the International Monetary Fund (IMF) hosted a conference at its headquarters in Washington, DC on rethinking economic policy. In his speech, Nobel Prize laureate in economics, George Akerlof, painted a vivid picture of the state of complexity facing the field of economics by comparing the economic crisis to a cat up a tree. The challenge was how to get the cat down from the tree.

He went on to describe a complex challenge in which every speaker had their own image of the cat, from their own perspective. Nobody had the same opinion, and each opinion was valid, but one thing was clear: *"we don't know what to do."*[39] In the words of another conference host and Noble Prize laureate Joseph Stiglitz: *"There is no good economic theory that explains why the cat is still up the tree."*

Not only do the greatest economists of our time not know what to do about the global financial crisis but also *"there is no agreed vision of what the future should look like,"* as Olivier Blanchard, the IMF chief economist, confessed.[40]

The language economists have recently used to describe the financial state of affairs in the world is markedly different from that preceding the financial crisis. The clear, confident messages have been replaced by a questioning, circumspect framing of the current challenges. They reveal the complexity of the terrain and the uncertainty of the way forward. As Blanchard put it, *"we are navigating by sight"* and *"we still do not know the final destination."*[41]

Yet knowing the final destination is a fallacy. The more complex the context, the harder it is to know where we are going to end up and what the outcomes will be. There are too many variables, too much uncertainty and ambiguity, and too many events that cannot be foreseen.

As psychologist Daniel Kahneman argues, *"Many people now say they knew a financial crisis was coming, but they didn't really. After a crisis we tell ourselves we understand why it happened and maintain the illusion that the world is understandable. In fact, we should accept the world is incomprehensible much of the time."*[42]

Planning and strategy are seen as a must in today's organizational life, but they perpetuate the illusion that we can work out a way forward that will take us safely to our final destination. Having a map to a largely unknown territory is as useful as having no map at all.

3.

COMPLICATED – COMPLEX – CHAOTIC

In February 2002, at a US Department of Defense news briefing on the absence of evidence on weapons of mass destruction in Iraq, Donald Rumsfeld, then US Secretary of Defence, famously quipped:

"There are known knowns; there are things we know that we know. There are known unknowns; that is to say, there are things that we now know we don't know. But there are also unknown unknowns – there are things we do not know we don't know."

In the context of a dry military briefing, this philosophical comment was so surreal that it became part of the vernacular and won him the Plain English Campaign's "Foot in the Mouth Award" in 2003. It is also a surprisingly accurate description of the challenges that we are facing in the modern world.

Welsh academic David Snowden's work on the nature of complex systems and their inherent uncertainty, "The Cynefin framework," is useful to look at here. Snowden distinguishes between four different domains:[45]

Simple
The domain of the "known knowns," characterized by the familiar, certain, and well-worn pathways

Example
- *The route I take to get to work*
- *How to make a chocolate cake*

Complicated
The domain of the "known unknowns," characterized by the ordered, predictable, forecastable; can be known by experts

Example
- *Applying current accounting rules*
- *Construction of a supertanker*
- *Restructuring an organization*

Complex
The domain of the "unknown unknowns," characterized by flux and unpredictability, no right answers, emergent instructive patterns, and many competing ideas

Example
- *Parenting teenagers,*
- *Developing a new product for a new market*
- *Forecasting the global economy*
- *Post-apartheid reconciliation*
- *Addressing social disadvantage*

Chaotic
The domain of the "unknowable unknowns," characterized by high turbulence and no patterns

Example
- *The events of 11 September 2001*
- *Bush fires*

WE LIVE IN VUCA

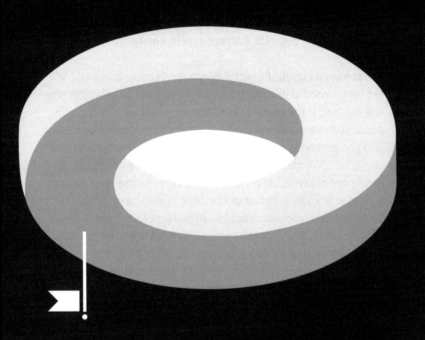

Snowden and fellow academic Mary Boone describe the difference between a complicated and a complex situation by comparing a Ferrari to a Brazilian rainforest. Ferraris are complicated machines with many moving parts that are themselves static. Although it might be impossible for you or me, an expert mechanic could take apart then reassemble a Ferrari given enough time. In contrast, a rainforest isn't made of static parts – the interplay between the tree canopy, the climate, the animals and insects, and the wider ecological and human social system is in constant flux. The whole is far more than the sum of its parts. While the Ferrari is complicated (ordered, predictable), the rainforest is complex (unpredictable, emergent).[46]

What trips us up in the world is not the "known knowns." We are pretty good at dealing with what we know. The solutions are self-evident. If the problem is a "known unknown," in the complicated domain, there is a solution that can eventually be found and the person with the best knowledge of the situation can sort it out. We can tackle the problems we know about by applying our expertise. If we don't have the expertise, we can find someone who does. Father of scientific management FW Taylor proposed that managers could analyze a problem, break it down into the parts, and improve incrementally to solve the problem. This reductionist thinking of organizations as machines can still be heard in popular language with metaphors, such as "this part of the organization needs fixing."

Traditional leadership thinking and practice, derived from Taylorism, that suggests that experts can solve the problem and leaders have the answers is not useful in the realm of "unknown unknowns." The command and control approach of the 20th century, with its reliance on efficiency, logic, quick decision-making and competence is only useful for tackling simple or complicated problems. Unfortunately this approach is totally inadequate in complex contexts. Complex challenges are characterized by the unexpected, the inconsistent and the inexplicable.

It is difficult enough to work out what the problem or question is, let alone the answer.

When talking about what it was like to engage with Russia during the Second World War, Winston Churchill said in a radio broadcast in October 1939: *"I cannot forecast to you the action of Russia. It is a riddle wrapped in a mystery inside an enigma."* This is a wonderful way to describe a complex, adaptive challenge.

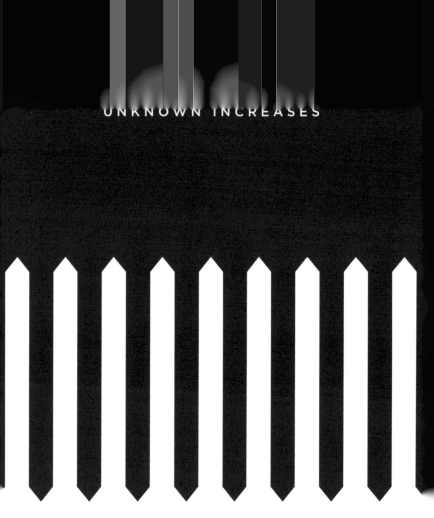

UNKNOWN INCREASES

KNOWLEDGE INCREASES

4.

MISHANDLING COMPLEXITY

"For every complex problem there is an answer that is clear, simple and wrong."

American journalist HL Mencken

Adaptive leadership faculty at Harvard University Kennedy School of Government Marty Linsky and Ronald Heifetz argue that misdiagnosing the complex (what they call "adaptive") elements of a challenge as complicated ("technical") is a key failure in leadership. We are trained to think technically and miss the adaptive. We are tempted to look for a silver bullet; an easy answer that will solve the problem in one go.

We see these "quick fixes" in many aspects of daily organizational life, like the current trend to dramatically restructure when we are not getting the results we want, or removing the person at the top of an organization. Also, under fear and stress of uncertainty, our brain will default to the old way of doing things because we are wired for habits, as neuroscientist Srini Pillay points out.[47]

A good example of this is the rapid replacement of CEOs or leaders within an organization after any sign of failure, often for things that are not even in their control or sphere of knowledge. In Fortune 500 companies the average tenure of a CEO is only 4.6 years; fragile and transient, this certainly is not long enough to establish long-term organizational or cultural change.

Quick fixes applied to complex problems are temporary solutions that don't engage with the issues deeply enough. They perpetuate the problem or aggravate it.

> *Steven: When I was working at an American investment bank in the role of VP, Diversity and Inclusion, I worked as part of a team on one of the bank's main challenges – to increase the number of women in senior management roles. This is a common challenge across many industries. Some companies respond to this by seeing it purely from a technical perspective. They provide communication skills or personal branding training, or change the recruitment process. The underlying issues that point to the adaptive nature of this challenge, such as the wider societal barriers to women rising to senior roles, or identifying the values and hidden assumptions held by different groups on this issue, are often not addressed.*
>
> *We began treating the issue as a complex adaptive challenge. Technical approaches made in conjunction with more sophisticated strategies, such as partnering with schools to raise awareness of the diversity of roles available, encouraging girls choosing exam subjects towards science, technology, mathematics and engineering, or organizing work placements and providing on-ramping solutions such as coaching for those returning to work from maternity leave. Many of these strategies don't provide an immediate solution but take on a more long-term approach by tackling the systemic issues at play at earlier or critical stages.*

In complex contexts the effects of our actions are unpredictable and the consequences cannot be fully understood in advance.

In the 1920s the American government enacted The National Prohibition Act, a nationwide ban on the sale of alcoholic beverages, in an attempt to eradicate the perceived negative effects of alcohol abuse on public life. The intent of the prohibition was to lower the consumption of alcohol and to make it seen unacceptable. While the consumption of alcohol halved during the prohibition, it had the unintended consequences of fuelling the growth of organized crime groups and creating an illegal alcohol industry. The organized crime groups took advantage of the fact that the consumption of alcohol was still popular, and produced unregulated, bootleg supply, which sometimes caused health problems. The growth in the illegal alcohol industry also increased the organized crime groups' business in other areas, leading to corruption and disregard of the law.

While the illegal alcohol industry flourished under the prohibition, the ban drove many small-time alcohol suppliers out of business and decimated the fledgling wine industry. Heavy drinkers and alcoholics found that support groups had withered away, and only found adequate support after the ban was lifted in 1933. Alcoholics Anonymous was founded in 1935. Also, before the prohibition era it was seen as socially unacceptable for women to drink in public, but with the newfound freedom after the prohibition ended, it became more common and bars opened catering for both men and women.

The prohibition is an example of how a law was passed to solve a complex social problem, and how there were many less-than-positive unintended consequences. This concept was popularized by American sociologist Robert K Merton, who argued that small, insignificant changes can have unintended, far-reaching and potentially devastating effects.

Not only do we not expect the unexpected, but we also tend to overestimate the control we will have in much more immediate or everyday actions. According to Harvard psychologist Ellen Langer, we suffer from an "illusion of control."[48]

Langer's research showed that we often think we have personal control in situations where there is none. For example, we may feel more confident that a car accident will not happen to us if we are the driver rather than the passenger. Also, where there is a "cue" of skill involved, we tend to behave as if we have control. For example, the gambler might feel his or her winning a game was influenced by his or her dexterity, where in fact the winning odds were no different, regardless of skill. Langer's research showed that traders who believed that they had more control over the markets actually performed worse.

So what happens when we can no longer rely on what we know, when we are forced to come face to face with the unknown?

PART II - THE EDGE

Finisterre

"The road in the end taking the path the sun had taken,
into the western sea, and the moon rising behind you
as you stood where ground turned to ocean: no way
to your future now but the way your shadow could take,
walking before you across water, going where shadows go,
no way to make sense of a world that wouldn't let you pass
except to call an end to the way you had come"

David Whyte

FINISTERRE

CHAPTER 4

1.

ARRIVING AT FINISTERRE

Cape Finisterre is often the final destination of *Il Camino*, the famous pilgrimage to the shrine of the apostle St James the Great in the Cathedral of Santiago de Compostela in Spain. Pilgrims walk a further 90km to reach the Cape, framed by steep cliffs dropping down to the Atlantic, also known in the Middle Ages as *"Mare Tenebrosum,"* or the dark sea. The beautiful, spectacular peninsula is aptly named *"finis terrae,"* Latin for *"the end of the world."*

Finisterre is the edge of everything known and familiar, a mysterious place. It separates our current reality, what we are comfortable with, from what is strange, unexplained, undiscovered and perhaps even undiscoverable. Behind us we have solid ground, the knowledge that got us so far. Ahead of us we have the unknown, the mysterious sea, unpredictable and uncontrollable. The fog is starting to settle and it is hard to see around us; the landscape is no longer familiar and there are no road signs or maps to show us the way.

In Roman times, when the map of the world was still being drawn, blank areas represented the unexplored vastness and contained the words "here be dragons," to warn explorers of the potential risks and dangers. Greek philosopher Plutarch described this space eloquently in his book *The Lives of the Noble Greeks and Romans* in the first century:

"As geographers ... crowd into the edges of their maps parts of the world which they do not know about, adding notes in the margin to the effect, that beyond this lies nothing but sandy deserts full of wild beasts, unapproachable bogs, Scythian ice, or a frozen sea, so, in this work of mine, ... I might very well say of those that are

farther off, beyond this there is nothing but prodigies and fictions, the only inhabitants are the poets and inventors of fables."

Just like those areas, what lies beyond the edge is waiting to be discovered. For some, this may be a sandy desert, for others muddy bogs or a frozen sea. The metaphor, the mental image that is conjured for each one of us will depend on our own story and experience at the edge. It may be a stark and wild place, an unfamiliar territory evoking strong sensations and reactions, or it may be a place for which we have a certain amount of excitement.

Finisterre is not just a one-time experience. We move through many edges, in a dynamic process that brings us face to face with both our limits and our possibilities. There are many situations that bring us to the edge: a loved one being diagnosed with a terminal illness, falling in love, starting a new job, or tackling a complex challenge, like leading an organization into a new market. It could be present in the form of a disruption, a crisis, a sudden change, making a mistake or failing at something important.

In spite of being in this situation many times before, we are never fully prepared for the moment when we arrive. Every edge is a new experience. Outside of our comfort zone, we experience a range of complex and conflicting emotions: from hesitation to avoidance and flight, excitement to terror, fear to boldness, and shame to vulnerability. We often fail to react well to standing at the edge. Our crafty brains play every trick in the book to keep us on dry land. We spend all our time trying to clamber back up the path, and we miss out on the learning that can only happen at Finisterre.

How we react at the edge – whether we choose to stay there or turn our backs and run – will determine whether our relationship with the unknown might be full of dread or full of potential. The edge is the crucial point where the future of our relationship with the unknown hangs in the balance.

Elitsa Dermendzhiskya, a young Bulgarian economist and social entrepreneur, travelled the Camino from France to Spain in
the summer of 2012, walking for nearly a month with little more
than a backpack.

*"What brought me to the path that day in early June was a sin I
needed to atone for – the sin of knowledge. As a mathematician
and economist by training, I readily subscribed to the notion of a
universe that could be measured, predicted and controlled. Not
only was it so neatly elegant, that notion, but it also perpetuated
the false sense of security that by applying the right theory one
could aspire to possess the Truth.*

*"Trouble was, I had taken the scientific credo to heart so much
that I tried to apply it in my personal life, substituting cost-benefit
analysis for intuition and crushing pleasure and spontaneity with
utility theory. My life turned into a sterile, mechanistic, perfectly
planned routine, the naïveté of which didn't quite register until
after my college graduation. Over time, my scientific façade was
stripped away, and I realized there was no absolute Truth to be
found; there was only my personal truth to be lived.*

*"To make the Camino experience as authentic as possible, I em-
braced a minimalist travelling style: no guidebook, no fancy GPS
mobile apps, no emergency equipment of any sort. Morning frost
or blistering sun, in the frequent drizzle and the occasional storm,
I'd be plodding along clad in shorts and a T-shirt. Some days I'd
trudge on for 50km of barren land, my feet blistered inside my
woollen socks.*

*"Besides the very literal uncertainty of walking the Camino, there
was another more personal level to it. People talked of visions and
divine revelations, of finding themselves – all claims that would
have me wincing before. I still had trouble imagining the skies
opening up to speak to me, but the power of intense silence and
walking to focus the mind's eye and to heighten one's self-awareness hadn't eluded me. I found myself both curious and scared of*

what would transpire. My fear was that deep down I was, in fact, a bad person.

"Halfway on the Camino I arrived in the village of Molinaseca one sweltering hot day in July. At its far end, two small tourist inns stood close by, and as I approached with the dozen or so other pilgrims, it was clear where everybody would set up camp for the night. New and shiny, made from smooth polished wood, the first inn was a far cry from the other – a dingy building whose owner might as well have come out of a horror movie set. Dishevelled hair, wild eyes, one missing leg, the unmistakable smell of spirits about him, the ominous screeching noises his cat made – those could only portend trouble. And yet I was drawn to that second inn on a gut level even though I 'knew' the danger.

"My feeling overriding my reason, I stayed – the only guest and scared beyond description but not wavering for a second. The inn keeper, perhaps out of gratefulness, went into his room and fished out a bottle of olive oil, which he handed to me with the words "only for special guests." Then we sat outside at the flimsy table and he told me his life story – a story of love and a happy marriage, a crippling accident in his mid-twenties, the ensuing treachery of the wife, the heartbreak, the denial, the anger at God and finally, the pilgrimage and the finding of God again. The man's name was Elisande. I had barely uttered a word the whole time, but when he finished his story, he told me, "You are a good person, Ellie."

"When people ask me what I found on the Camino, I always feel tempted to say, 'That I'm a good person'. I never say it, of course. I went out searching for my truth and I think this scary man brought me closer to it."

2.
AVOIDING THE UNKNOWN

"There is nothing that man fears more than the touch of the unknown. He wants to see what is reaching toward him and to be able to recognize or at least classify it. Man always tends to avoid physical contact with anything strange."

Author Elias Canetti

Diana: *"Where should we begin?", I ask the leadership team of a large not-for-profit. Twenty pairs of eyes stare back at me. The question is not rhetorical. This is often the first question I ask at the start of a leadership development programme. It is meant to uncover the expectations that are placed on people in an authority position, in situations high in uncertainty and complexity. Expectations that are normal, but that often get in the way of learning and growth. Although deceptively simple, this question always takes the group right to the edge.*

*"You are asking **us** this question? Surely you know the answer, you are running this programme." I say nothing and look around the room. "Start at the beginning," quips a woman right in front of me. I keep silent, and sit down.*
"Start with the end in mind," says another.
The suggestions are starting to come thick and fast now.
"Where it makes sense."

"With the agenda. How can we start without knowing what we are going to be working on over the next few days?"

"Are we clear on the purpose?"

"What about going round the room and hearing from everyone what they think?"

"Does it matter?"

"How will we decide?" asks a man to my right.

I continue to be silent.

I can sense the group starting to get impatient. Some people are shifting in their chairs, others are looking at me, waiting to see what I do.

I do nothing. "What do you want from us?" says a young woman in an exasperated voice.

"I'm more interested in what you want from me," I answer.

I am not fulfilling the traditional, expected role of the person at the front of the room, and without a task and clear direction, the disequilibrium in the group is quickly increasing.

"I'm feeling frustrated, I don't know what the goal is."

"Why don't you just take us on the journey?"

"There is no leadership here, no direction!" complains someone.

In the absence of a clear structure, the conversation starts feeling circular and confusing.

After a while, silence descends on the group. All eyes are on me, waiting for me to do something. Although I've been in this situation before, the silence feels heavy and uncomfortable. I feel tempted to say something, but I hold steady. The void gets filled quickly.

"This won't work in a large group like this. We'll never agree to one answer. Let's break into small groups and brainstorm," suggests one of the more senior men in the group. There is an almost audible sigh of relief. Finally, something to do. The more structure-oriented people are immediately attracted to this proposal. They are starting to move their chairs, but there are some people in the group who are holding back, waiting for what will happen next. As there is no consensus in the group, nothing happens.

"If we don't have a framework, we're lost."

"I feel like we're poking around in the dark."

Someone cracks a joke and the whole group laughs uproariously. The tension dissipates for a few moments, but is short lived.
"It feels like we're on the wrong track, but we don't know what the right track is."
I sense some people's frustration now is going to a new level. Some people are leaning back in their chairs, looking absent or lost. A few people start talking amongst themselves, and I notice a couple are checking their phones.
"There's nothing worse than this happening in a meeting... take the lead!" shouts a man to my left.
Time seems to slow down. I can hear the ticking of the clock on the wall. I don't think I have much time now. I stand up, take the whiteboard marker, and start debriefing the session.

When we step into a new space, where we are faced with an uncertain and complex task, we inevitably come to the edge of our competence. We can recognize we are at the edge if there are changes in the energy of the situation - embarrassed laughter, fidgeting or boredom; if information is missing or keeps being repeated; or if there is nervousness, feelings of getting lost or not knowing what to do next[49]. When the disequilibrium increases, we naturally fall back on what we know. To avoid the uncomfortable feelings that arise outside of our comfort zone, we resort to tried and tested ways of organizing a group, designing an agenda or creating some structure. We look to those in decision-making roles to restore the equilibrium and provide us with clarity and safety. Otherwise we blame them for not 'showing leadership', or we disengage altogether from the current situation, finding other things to occupy us.

What is behind this avoidance of the unknown?

3.

FEAR OF INCOMPETENCE

"I feel the pressure to look competent whilst inside I'm drowning," says a senior manager in government. *"For me, respect is the ultimate. I am worried that if I look incompetent, I will lose people's respect. I will lose my credibility. Without credibility I can't influence the outcome. The fear of looking incompetent holds me back from fully participating."*

Feelings of incompetence commonly arise at the edge. Facing our gap in knowledge can lead to questioning who we are, our competence, confidence, professionalism, knowledge and power. Nicola Gatti, CEO of startup AWS24, has spent almost all his career in the telecommunications industry. He describes a situation when he recently moved to the financial sector as a mergers and acquisitions director and found out that he had a serious gap in his professional knowledge.

"On the cusp of my first international tender, my direct boss asked me: what WACC are you using in the Business Plan? OK, I barely knew how to read a Business Plan, but 'WACC'? I had to ask one of my collaborators: 16% he said, and I reported this figure to my boss, I still remember it. It was such an embarrassing feeling for me! Like when you're thrown into the water and don't know how to swim: having to manage a complex tender with incomplete knowledge.

"Over time, I came to learn all the ropes, and even the tricks, of corporate finance, but most of all, I learnt how to manage a situation in the face of uncertainty, and still be successful: we won that tender, and several others afterwards."

During that intense period, Nicola learned that no human being can be an expert in all fields. The best strategy has to be built by necessity in the presence of imperfect knowledge. This lesson has accompanied him throughout his professional career.

There are many assumptions we have about what might happen if we admit we don't know. Some of them are well founded and some are not. The dangers of appearing not to do a job well, not to have sufficient expertise, of not knowing enough are real. We can lose our benefits, influence, authority, even our job. The consequences of not fulfilling our responsibilities, our objectives, are always in the background. A senior manager in the health sector explains: *"I am worried that I won't be respected if I don't know. I want to get it right. I am known for getting it right, and getting to the answer quickly. Do you know what will happen if I slow things down? I run the risk of letting down the reputation I have built for efficient delivery. People are counting on me. There is a lot at stake."*

Diana: In my early days as a lawyer I struggled with feelings of incompetence: "Every time someone asks 'how is the project going?' in a well-meaning way, I feel sick. Just that simple question, asked naively, brings up all my insecurities and doubts in one go. And every time I am tempted to pretend it's all going fine. Fine. Great. But it occurs to me that this is the point where we've all been before. The point where we can pretend we are OK, in control, achieving what we've set out to achieve, or we can be open and honest with how it really is (hard) and how we're feeling (not good). Actually, bad, very bad. The point where I could just reveal that the only thing that I know is that I actually don't know!" This became a repetitive experience. I noticed that the higher the stakes, the harder it was to admit I didn't know. What stopped me from acknowledging that I was struggling? It was the fear of looking and sounding incompetent. I was convinced that revealing my true feelings would in some way diminish me and undermine my status. The stuckness I was feeling in my work was now being perpetuated in my interactions and relationships. The more closed I became about my insecurities, the more I felt like a fraud. I'd given all the power away to an external 'judge' who was assessing my worthiness based on how I was going in my work.

One reason we fear the unknown is that we are brought face to face with ourselves and our own fragility, our mortality. We are not infallible after all. When we are well within our comfort zone, dealing with situations and problems that are familiar and questions that have an answer, we feel full of mastery and agency. Our roles, both formal and informal, protect us from the unknown, but they can also get in the way of us fully engaging with it.

Roles are like a protective cloak that we can hide behind to avoid the vulnerability of Not Knowing. They are protective because we can rely on them to pretend we know, as everyone is looking to us for an answer. It's easy, at least on the surface, to succumb to the pressure and provide an answer. With a cloak we are not exposed. We can rely on the structures and processes around us, the lists and plans we create to give the impression of order, control and certainty. In time this becomes a habit. Wearing the defensive cloak of knowledge becomes so second nature that we forget we are wearing a mantle of defence. We've become the cloak and we've lost ourselves in it. The cloak becomes a straitjacket. Like the emperor with no clothes, everyone pretends not to notice. Nobody dares state the obvious: that the emperor is naked. There are no answers. We are vulnerable in our incompetence.

People report feeling conflict between their inner experience of Not Knowing and the outer situation, with its demands of maintaining the impression of competence.

This experience is shared by Reka Czegledi-Brown, an organizational consultant for almost 20 years. A few years ago she was engaged by a local government authority to facilitate integration with a public health department. Even though she was reluctant to set herself up as the expert, the client insisted that she provide detailed information on her professional background. She was told that "*as this situation is so sensitive, we can't afford to have someone who has no idea.*" From the outset her client's expectations were for her to solve their problems. She felt a strong pressure to know and "save the day." This placed the responsibility squarely on her shoulders and relieved her client of the anxiety of Not Knowing. Even though she brought considerable experience to the job, she initially found herself paralyzed by a high level of uncertainty and doubt. But this was not something the client was prepared to hear.

It took Reka a few months to re-orient her client's expectations. She did this by making the work the primary focus for the client. *"It wasn't about me,"* she says. *"It was about truly deeply listening to them and being with them during this difficult transition. They were so unbelievably lost and 'unseen', not fully acknowledged. It was such a painful position to be in that my willingness to engage and be there with them was a big step. I made myself vulnerable rather than reverting to expertise and hiding behind it."*

To feel incompetent, useless or inadequate is very uncomfortable. Admitting Not Knowing can be a disempowering experience because it means experiencing a loss of power and control, which in turn can lead to acute feelings of embarrassment and shame.

Common reactions in the workplace:
"I'd rather not have all this attention"
"I made a mistake and I feel that I want to die"
"I can't try this, I'm no good at it"
"If I was a good manager I wouldn't have let that happen"
"I should know what to do. Something's wrong with me"
"I can't let anyone know about this mistake, my credibility is at stake"
"How could I be so stupid?"

One of the common signs that we have arrived at the edge is the feeling of being embarrassed by our limitations. We do not want to look bad or lose public esteem. This experience that "all eyes are on us" can take the form of mild shyness, where the most obvious sign may be that we feel self-conscious. At the other end of the spectrum we may experience a harsh inner criticism and feelings of shame, which can be deeply painful and isolating.

Shame is the feeling that "I am wrong," in which our very identity is threatened, not simply our actions. Brené Brown, a researcher into vulnerability and shame, defines shame as *"the intensely painful feeling or experience of believing we are flawed and therefore unworthy of love and belonging."*[50] One of the ways we can recognize shame is by the sense of isolation it triggers. It can prevent us from moving forward as we want to get away from the people and the situation that are making us feel this way. Shame prohibits us from wanting to express our views about the situation at all.

The inner critic emerges at the edge; resembling the voice of reason and logic, this critic throws doubt at our ability to do something and it holds us back.

> *Diana: When I began a role managing the refugee centre of a large social organization, I faced up to a formidable inner critic: "The inner critic casts its dark shadow. I heard its voice in my head loud and clear: 'You can't do this! You are so foolish to have even thought that you could succeed. You are too big for your boots and now everyone can see you for who you are. The job is too high-level for you and you don't have enough experience. Everyone else is so much more experienced and talented. They've had years of training and they know so much more than you do.'*

> *"Doubt has settled in. It's warm and reassuring in a disturbing way. I've been here before, where I start worrying and become soft and floppy like a rag doll. I don't feel like doing anything. I can't find the energy. My thoughts are floating in a mushy sea of half-*

*frozen ice. I am confused about where I am or what I am supposed
to be doing. I don't know where to begin. It's overwhelming."*

Professor Carol Dweck, a world-leading researcher of motivation at Stanford University, sought to understand why it is that some people succeed while others don't. She was very interested in finding out whether there was a correlation between intelligence, talent and success.

In her book *Mindset* Dweck published some startling findings from her research: that mindset makes more of a difference to success than ability does.[51] This is the self-narrative that we tell ourselves – about our intelligence, our ability to learn, our personality and our talents. It shapes whether we stick to what we know, or whether we enter into the unknown and develop new skills.

Dweck distinguishes between two basic mindsets. A fixed mindset is where we believe that our intelligence, talents and traits are fixed at birth. They are the inheritance of our genes, our cultural conditioning, or the way in which we have been parented. This is a fixed idea, that even though we may be able to make incremental improvement, it is unlikely we will ever be able to change that much. In contrast, a growth mindset is one in which we believe that although we have a starting point with our natural talents, traits and intelligence, we can develop further, cultivate our traits and improve our talents through sheer practice, discipline and persistence to achieve our goals.

Steven: An example of a fixed mindset is my attitude to maths. As a child I never excelled at maths. For others it came naturally but I had to really struggle in class. I told myself: "I'm just the type of person who is good at writing and the humanities. I am not a maths or science person. Some people are just more numerate than others." This mindset was only challenged when I was 16 and decided to do the subject for A-level. Getting a low grade however, seemed only to convince me of my belief. The negative consequence is that I later avoided job applications or even study that required high numeracy skills, even though they may have led to jobs that I wanted.

An example of a growth mindset is the first time I played table tennis with my brother Selwyn, I was terrible. We used our school books as a make-shift net and our kitchen table. Yet by playing regularly with my brother and also our dad, who was much better than both of us, I kept improving my technique. By the time I was 18, I was good enough to represent my university in competitive matches.

Whether we have a fixed or growth mindset has significant implications for the choices we make, our behaviour and therefore for our results. For example, Dweck argues that those who have a fixed mindset need to constantly prove themselves and confirm to themselves and others their capability. They do everything to avoid the unknown, which they believe may result in failure. According to Dweck, every situation is evaluated for a binary outcome: "Will I succeed or fail?" "Will I be a winner or a loser?" With this mindset we avoid tasks we are not sure we will be good at. We may want to be flawless the first time we try something and if we have deficiencies, we will naturally want to hide them. Failure for a fixed mindset type of person can lead to shame. They may also seek to surround themselves with people who can make them look good, rather than those against whom they may not measure up. A fixed mindset is a critical stumbling block at the edge. It stops us from being open to trying new things and experimenting.

4.

REACTIONS AT THE EDGE

Sometimes it is hard to know when we are at the edge. Complex problems don't arrive at our front door wrapped and labelled so that we can easily recognize them. The way we react at the edge can give us clues about when we are entering the unknown.

There are many ways in which we avoid the unknown. When we come close to something we do not understand, or are faced with something unexpected or inexplicable, we have a tendency to control, become passive and withdraw, analyze things endlessly, resort to catastrophic thinking (in which we assume that everything will always turn out for the worst), jump into action, getting busy or apply quick fixes. We marginalize the experience because it disturbs us too much. These are natural and mostly unconscious ways in which we cope with the discomfort experienced at the edge – a result of our survival instincts going back to the origins of the human species. The problem with this, however, is that we avoid the unknown just at the times when we would really benefit from embracing it. Our avoidance can often prevent us from staying at the edge of the unknown, and ultimately it can prevent our learning.

Common visceral reactions: [52]
"I get a knot in my stomach"
"It's like something is pressing on my head, waiting to burst out"
"My heart goes 100 miles an hour"
"I get slightly dizzy"
"I start sweating"
"My mouth gets dry, my voice starts cracking"
"I become giggly, like I'm slightly drunk"
"I get fidgety, I can't sit still"

Common language often heard in the workplace:
"I feel that I have nothing to stand on anymore. Losing the contract was a significant loss for my team"
"The take-over created such change it was literally as if the earth moved overnight. People are acting very differently today than they were yesterday"
"It's like we're poking around in the dark"
"Since losing my job, I feel as if things have fallen apart"
"Everyday something changes around here. If it's one initiative today, by tomorrow there's a new one in its place. Nothing feels solid anymore"
"Just starting my new role feels very messy. There's nothing to hold onto"

Buddhist nun and teacher Pema Chödrön describes the experience at the edge as "groundlessness." It is as though a carpet has been pulled out from under our feet. With nothing solid to stand on, we can feel disoriented, confused and even panicked or terrified.

Alex Schlotterbeck, a trainee psychotherapist, describes the myriad emotions she felt when she was in between jobs.

"I get in touch with the angst of Not Knowing where the money for the next mortgage payment is coming from as I bridge the gap from one job to the next. I get in touch with the anxiety of the uncertainty. I get in touch with my pessimistic predictions when faced with Not Knowing what's next for me and the times when I have slipped into feeling depressed. There is some comfort in the certainty of feeling down rather than the anxiety of Not Knowing. I get in touch with not being able to bear Not Knowing and so trying to take control of my life by anxiously moving away too quickly."

Control
Feelings of mastery, agency, autonomy and control are important and are connected with our sense of wellbeing.

FINITE IS THE EDGE OF THE KNOWN

Neuroscientist David Rock's work shows that when employees experience a lack of control or agency, their perception of uncertainty is also aroused, which further raises their stress levels. By contrast, the perception of greater autonomy increases the feeling of certainty and reduces stress.[53]

Psychologist Ellen Langer, whose research on the "illusion of control" we referred to earlier (see page 93), argues that our tendency to believe we can control or influence outcomes is strengthened by stressful and competitive situations. When things are changing and becoming more unpredictable, stress levels rise and we feel more at the mercy of our circumstances. It is then that we attempt to increase our sense of control and relieve our sense of powerlessness. Control appears as a defence, an antidote to Not Knowing; a grasp for certainty. We can experience ourselves tightening or closing down. Or we can apply more power and become more directive and authoritarian. The language we use for these situations is apt: we "tighten the screws" or "lock things down."

Common reactions:
"I start pressuring myself even more to come up with the answer"
"I get really impatient with my team"
"I jump into action and take over"
"I will do anything to avoid being uncomfortable"
"I'm intellectualizing the feelings to manage them"
"I'm drowning"
"I'm so out of control"
"I completely lost control of that meeting"
"I'm going off track"

Pema Chödrön says there is a tendency to *"scramble for security... and gain some ground."* She calls this "Shenpa," which is a Tibetan word for attachment.

Chödrön describes Shenpa as having a *"visceral quality associated with grasping, or conversely, pushing away... It's that stuck feeling, that tightening or closing down or withdrawing we experience when we're uncomfortable with what's going on."*[54]

When the pressure is on, our default position is to control through routines and familiar structures and rules. Organizations create artificial structures to give the illusion of control. Motorola's Six Sigma management strategy, a set of techniques and tools for manufacturing process improvement, is a manifestation of our desire to control our environment. While it can be effective for simple or complicated (known unknown) problems, many business problems are complex (unknown unknowns). It is an illusion that we can achieve stable and predictable outcomes in business and "mistake-proof" activities by applying common business systems to the unknown unknowns. Will this new product work? What direction are customer tastes and preferences moving in? What unpredictable forces will have an impact on us?

Passivity & self-defeat
Common reactions:
"I become too accommodating, agreeing with whatever is being suggested"
"I become really quiet and withdrawn"
"I don't know what questions to ask"
"If I am not 100% sure, I'll tend to sit and become silent, especially if I don't have the detail backing me"
"I look to my manager to do something. After all, it's his responsibility"
"I lose my confidence"
"My brain feels like it is in sleep mode"
"I can blame myself and others"

When we are faced with a sense of groundlessness, one of our default responses is to move away from our feelings and to isolate ourselves using worry or depression. The problem seems catastrophic and we don't know what to do or how to cope. We tend to want to escape from the place that scares us, which is a natural human reaction. The mix of uncomfortable feelings and reactions is strong and we can easily be pulled into the feeling of despair.

Analysis paralysis

Common reactions:
"We need to form a committee to discuss this"
"We don't have enough data to make a decision"
"We need more information before I'm happy to sign off"
"I'd like to read the report by ABC consulting that comes out next month before we go ahead with the rollout"

We often avoid tackling a complex problem by trying to analyze and gather more information. We erroneously think that our difficulty with solving a complex problem is due to our lack of knowledge. If only we read more, researched more, became better at our jobs, we would be able to come up with the answer. The challenge with this thinking is that when we are dealing with a complex challenge, which may well be difficult to define, let alone solve, we may never get to the bottom of it. We may never know enough, or become competent enough to be able to solve it. The risk is that by the time the analysis is complete, the problem has changed shape, become too entrenched, or it is simply not a problem any more, thus rendering all our planning redundant.

Over-analyzing can be a way to procrastinate and avoid action because it is a comfortable, known way to tackle a problem. However, as Nicola Gatti, CEO of AWS24, learned: *"It is better to move on with imperfect knowledge, based on your capacities and instincts, than to wait for knowledge. This is preferable even though you could miss some valuable chances in this fast-moving world."*

Catastrophic thinking

Catastrophic thinking is exaggerating the consequences of a problem and defaulting to the "worst-case scenario" of what could possibly go wrong. Not only do we dislike the experience, we believe that we are unable to cope or do anything to change it.

Common reactions

"I will never get out of this situation"
"I've got it wrong and now all is lost"
"They'll see how dumb I am and I'll lose people's confidence in me"
"If I lose this contract the company will fold"
"I have totally lost my mind. I can't think straight. I'm such a failure"
"How can I show my face at work tomorrow? I would rather die!"

Karen Loren,[55] a management consultant, describes a time when she was feeling stuck in an unfulfilling role and was searching for what might reignite her passion:

"Drowning in thoughts about the future, I got caught up in a cycle of desperately searching for jobs and feelings of panic from not knowing what I wanted. Despair and panic soon took up residence in my thoughts and my gut was plagued by a persistent ache. My imagination went wild with the fear. I had visions of jumping feet first into a totally new field and ending up homeless because it all went horrendously wrong. I fantasized about reaching retirement and still not having figured it all out."

Jumping into action

Common reactions:

"We were managing the anxiety of Not Knowing by throwing all our knowledge and expertise at it"
"We kept coming up with plan after plan, rushing from one task to another like headless chooks"
"What's the point of meeting and leaving without a clear set of actionable tasks?"
"We got stuck down the rabbit hole of expertise by brainstorming the problem to death"
"I don't have time to play with questions. We are here to get a job done, and quickly"

Making decisions may promise immediate gratification. The rush of relief that can come straight after a decision has been made may be similar to a hit of sugar. It can initially give us a boost, but it can eventually take us further "down" than where we first started. Many workplaces have a low tolerance to uncertainty, so we apply "a 30-second rush to value." We tend to intellectualize the problem and lower the discomfort of Not Knowing by providing superficial answers. Feeling overwhelmed by the prospect of appearing incompetent, we succumb to the pressure to act. A human resources manager in the insurance industry explains:

"I alleviate the discomfort of Not Knowing through over-thinking. I need to appear competent in my area of expertise. I am expected to know and I expect to have the answer. I become even more impatient, rushing through decisions, fixated on the outcomes."

Resistance
How does resistance feel?
"I can feel it in my body"
"I get headaches, like a vice, a force that pushes on my head"
"There is a heaviness on my chest, I can't breathe"
"I feel a pressure, constraining me, locking me down"
"It is a limiting belief about myself"
"I feel stuck. The more I struggle, the more stuck I get"
"For me it's like I'm wading through murky waters or thick mud"
"It's like I've come to a dead end"

Resistance is a pushing away of the present, usually as a reaction to change and the loss associated with change. It could be resistance to something that is unpleasant or negative, something that we fear or dislike or is too difficult to see. When we are resisting, we are wishing for things to be different.

Author Nick Williams left a successful corporate life in which he appeared to have everything he wanted because he felt something was missing. After nine years in three corporate jobs in his

20s, he felt an impulse to leave and start his own business. That was before the Internet, and before social media and downshifting and the idea of portfolio careers.

"I felt like I would be stepping off the edge of the world I knew if I did that, committing career suicide, letting everyone down after I had worked so hard to get where I was. I feared I would become alienated. I had always followed the rules, played a role and done what I thought I was supposed to, but it wasn't making me happy."

Nick recalls a moment, almost 10 years later, when his resistance came up strongest, after signing his first book contract and becoming a writer. Since childhood he had a sense that writing was something he was born to do, a part of his calling. However, at 38 years old he had not written a single book.

In the summer of 1997, he had been germinating ideas around the theme of finding and living the work "you are born to do." He was beginning to do workshops and talks on this theme, and a book seemed like a natural next step. He decided to submit a proposal to the six largest publishers in the UK, and to his surprise, one publisher asked to meet with him. Nick was glad that he had taken action, but a deep-seated part of him did not believe he would be successful. He had heard too many stories of crushing rejection letters, or worse still, no reply at all.

On 1 September 1998, a letter fell through his letterbox onto the carpet. Nick remembers picking it up and seeing the publisher's logo on the envelope. Suddenly he was filled with a great fear of rejection. He opened it quickly to get it over and done with. He wanted to confirm that he was not good enough, but congratulate himself in a perverse way that at least he had tried. As he opened the letter, he was stunned. It said *"Congratulations, we are happy to offer you a contract for your book." "I was speechless and had a moment of elation. But then the 'dragons' I call my resistance surfaced. I had thoughts such as 'what have you done!? You can't write and you've made a mess by convincing people you can', 'who will read anything you write, surely the books will end up in the remainder bin'. I even thought to myself 'I can't write, what if it's terrible and it's even wasting trees'. Such was the strong voice of my resistance."*

Change always involves loss. We do everything we possibly can to avoid loss, even if it means achieving something we've always dreamed of. Not Knowing becomes even more frightening at the edge because we don't know what we are about to step into and what we are leaving behind.

THE ILLUSION
OF CONTROL

5.

THE CALL TO CROSS THE EDGE

Have you ever sensed something rising up from deep within yourself, a slow rumble of dissatisfaction with the status quo? This can push through the avoidance, urging us to follow the unknown. American mythologist Joseph Campbell depicts this sense of longing as a "call," the moment when we realize that life as it is cannot continue in the same way. Whether we like it or not, we must face the beginnings of change and cross the edge into the unknown.

When London-based coach Aboodi Shabi heard the "call" for change, he felt that he could no longer ignore or resist it. A few years ago, after several happy years living in central London, he began to realize that he was missing something – the quiet and peace of the West Country that he had left behind some years ago. At first, he just accepted this as a compromise he was willing to make. Living in the heart of London made sense in many ways, so he was ready to accept the price he had to pay. But whenever he spent time in the countryside, he would feel pangs of longing and nostalgia for nature. For a while, he was able to put them to one side and get on with his normal life.

However, things changed one spring when he went on a retreat in Italy. He had time and space to really listen and he rested and immersed himself in the beauty of spring in the Italian countryside, spending his days in the warm sunshine, listening to birds singing, and walking in the forest. In the evenings, reading by an open fire, he started to realize that he could no longer ignore the call.

"I immediately felt a lot of confusion. How could I leave London? Where would I go? How would I set about making the changes? My mind went to all the usual places. I tried to figure out 'the

solution' and struggled with the sense of uncertainty and the knowledge that there would be no easy answers. However, instead of trying to work it all out by myself, I called one of my friends in London to discuss my dilemma. His advice was challenging: 'it's not up to you to figure it out – you can't be in charge of how life unfolds'."

Aboodi returned to London, both excited and disturbed. He was aware now that life wouldn't just go on as before. Even though nothing had changed, he was already entering a transition phase. He tried to put his friend's advice into practice and whenever he got caught in trying to fathom out what to do, or worrying about how he would reconcile what felt like opposite parts of himself, he would try to just meditate, or go for a walk or a bike ride. One of the things he found especially helpful was realizing that whilst he didn't know how the path would unfold, he would know the answer in 10 or 15 years' time. Meanwhile he decided that he could enjoy the process of finding out what he needed to know. Whilst that didn't necessarily make the situation any easier, it did open up a mood of curiosity and wonder to accompany the uncertainty and disruption that he was experiencing.

Nearly two years later, Aboodi found a temporary resting station along the journey. He sold his flat in central London and moved into rented accommodation near the woods in a quiet North London suburb.

"In some ways, life is more unsettled than it was before. New challenges have arisen. My work life is changing, partly because I've realized that I no longer want to travel as much as I used to. My landlord comes back next year and I will have to move again, and property prices are rising fast. But what I am increasingly aware of, in the midst of all the unsettledness, is that I am becoming more settled. I am more at peace with Not Knowing. My intermittent meditation practice has become a daily habit. I walk or run in the woods near my house most days, and I have started regular yoga classes. I'm still no nearer to figuring out what to do, but the

practices are supporting me in staying more serene as I tread the path of the unknown."

As we become aware of our default reactions at the edge, we can deliberately choose to leave them behind and cultivate new skills and capabilities – conscious ways of playing at the edge. Like the Olympic gymnast, we need to practise these approaches to ensure that when the nerves and uncomfortable feelings hit us, we don't revert to bad habits but rather stay open to the many possibilities that lie ahead.

> **Diana:** *Just before I resigned from a job I felt an internal tension that was saying on the one hand "tread carefully, hold back," while on the other there was a curiosity that was nudging me forward. "I wonder what's around the corner? Should I keep going? The tension is palpable... If I go beyond the initial, automatic reaction of fear, if I stay with the discomfort, the panic, the knot in the stomach, as I look down from the edge, into the abyss, I can sense an invitation, a gentle beckoning, a slight pull to the unknown. If I allow those feelings to settle, I discover a sense of excitement. This is what those explorers venturing into unknown territory, no longer on the map, must have been feeling – a mixture of dread and excitement. A tug of war between the head and the heart. A sense of aliveness, where all the senses are engaged fully."*

We have made it this far. Are we ready for the next part of the journey – playing at the edge and dipping our toes into the uncharted waters of the unknown? Perhaps even venturing further than we've ever ventured before... Possibility and learning are just around the corner.

As poet David Whyte encourages in his poem *Finisterre*, let's

"... abandon the shoes that had brought you here
right at the water's edge, not because you had given up
but because now, you would find a different way to tread,
and because, through it all, part of you could still walk on,
no matter how, over the waves."

DARKNESS ILLUMINATES

CHAPTER 5

DARKNESS IS YOUR CANDLE

Persian poet and Sufi mystic Rumi

1.

A REFRAMING OF NOT KNOWING

When we first shared the idea of a book on Not Knowing with people, the feedback tended to be negative:

"What's good about not knowing things?"
"I don't see any benefit in ignorance"
"I'd prefer to know people than not know them"
"Not knowing means I'm vulnerable, I can get cheated on if I'm naïvé"
"Why would I want to look illiterate, a buffoon in front of others?"
"I'm lost enough as it is, why would I want to get more lost?"

It follows that if knowing is good, then its opposite is bad. It's a simple matter of logic for most people. But when we use the term Not Knowing we aren't talking about the common view of those two words, but rather the ancient "apophatic tradition" used to describe what something was "not" rather than what it was. In this spirit we are distinguishing Not Knowing from the position of the absence of knowledge (otherwise known as ignorance), and from partial knowledge that can be discovered.

A common contemporary metaphor associates knowledge with light and Not Knowing with darkness. This is illustrated by the phrase "I'm in the dark." Paradoxically, Not Knowing often leads to learning and new knowledge. Just as in nature and biology, Not Knowing can lead to growth that is unseen, like the embryo in the womb or the seed deep in the earth.

We are tempted to think that nothing is happening when it is not easily visible, yet transformation is unfolding, in the dark. We tend to place more value on the seen, things in the metaphorical light, but nature presents a perfect balance of day and night. Admitting that we don't know allows us to learn. The darkness of Not Knowing creates the freedom and space for new sources of illumination.

In *The Art of Looking Sideways*, Alan Fletcher describes the idea of space as "substance," rather than void. He gives the example of many artists who created works of art through making space for art to emerge from. For example, Cézanne, who painted and modelled space, Giacometti who sculpted by "taking the fat off space," Ralph Richardson who used pauses in acting, and Isaac Stern who composed music with silences.[56] In a similar way, the absence of knowledge in Not Knowing is a "negative" space full of potential.

The problem with the "positive" side of knowledge is that it can often crowd out the opportunities presented in the "negative," Not Knowing space. People in Vesalius' time couldn't admit that perhaps Galen didn't know everything there was to know about anatomy. For 1,400 years that belief crowded out the possibility to question, to see with new eyes, and therefore to learn new things and create new knowledge. The "knowledge" implied in former US president George W Bush's assertion of "Mission Accomplished", after the initial phase of the second Gulf War in Iraq, crowded out the possibility that it was not (accomplished). His "forthright" leadership was so unequivocal that there was no possibility of doubt. Yet doubt would have allowed more of a learning approach, which could have enabled the allies to enter Iraq with open minds about what would work, rather than assuming that military might was the solution.

Prior to the global financial crisis of 2008, the common belief was that all the major businesspeople and politicians had enough knowledge of the economy to be able to make rational decisions and properly factor in the risks of their investments. Gordon Brown, the former Chancellor of the Exchequer and later Prime Minister in England, had earlier proudly claimed *"An end to boom and bust."* This was later proven to be largely incorrect.

We are not talking about situations where we can know or we should know. Not Knowing doesn't mean that we put aside everything that we already know. By entering Not Knowing, we enter a space where we are not constrained by existing knowledge. Not Knowing is a way of engaging with situations, where the way forward is not knowable, or tackling complex problems that do not have an answer. Not Knowing is an active process, a choice to open up to new experiences and learning. It is a way of living and working with complexity, ambiguity and paradox, tolerating uncertainty and the uncomfortable feelings that we notice at the edge. This view challenges the negative connotations of Not Knowing and reframes Not Knowing as a positive space of potential and opportunity, where we can access new, emergent knowledge.

TRANSFORMATION

IS UNFOLDING

IN THE DARK

2.

WHAT CAN WE LEARN FROM THE INHABITANTS OF THE UNKNOWN?

Mounted on a granite block, an imposing statue stands at City Square on the corner of Collins and Swanston Streets in Melbourne, Australia.

The inscription around the base reads:
Robert O'Hara Burke and William John Wills
Leaders of the Victorian exploring expedition
The first to cross the continent from south to north
They perished on the return journey
At Cooper's creek, Central Australia, June 1861

Burke stands to the left of the seated Wills, arm resting on his shoulder. A book lies open in Wills' lap. The statue was unveiled on 21 April 1865, four years after the expedition's ill-fated end.

The story of Burke and Wills is one of triumph, as the expedition managed to reach the Gulf of Carpentaria on the northern coast of Australia – a journey of 3,000km. It is also a story of disaster because many lives were lost along the way. Burke and Wills only made it back to Cooper's Creek, less than one-third of the way back to Melbourne, where, at their deserted supply camp, they died of starvation.

Many historians have asked themselves how could Burke and Wills have died of starvation when they were surrounded by bush food (or "bush tucker" as it is called in Australia), rich sources of native foods used by the indigenous people living in the outback?[57] As Ian Clark, author of *The Aboriginal Story of Burke and Wills: Forgotten Narratives* comments, whilst the Europeans were perishing, the Aborigines were thriving.[58] The book argues that the answer to this question lies in Burke's attitude. He had little respect, bordering on disdain, for the indigenous people and their knowledge of the land. Other explorers had used indigenous trackers in previous expeditions and the failure of this expedition is attributed to the lack of Aboriginal guides. The inability, or unwillingness, of the explorers to meaningfully engage with the local inhabitants of the land led to their demise.

Burke had left one of his men, William Brahe, in charge of the supply depot at Cooper's Creek and he ordered him to prevent any Aborigines from coming close to the depot. Returning from the Gulf of Carpentaria after four months, Burke, Wills and King had missed Brahe by a few hours; he had given up waiting and abandoned the camp earlier that day.

Ian Clark believes that if Brahe had encouraged good relationships with the Yandruwandha people, who had lived in the Cooper's Creek area for thousands of years, they would have been able to inform him of the imminent arrival of Burke and his party. Likewise, if Burke had not rejected contact with the Yandruwandha, they could have sent word further down the track to let Brahe know that they were coming.[59]

Once at Cooper's Creek, the explorers distrusted the Yandruwandha people's offers of friendship and hospitality. In his diary Wills described the tribes as "*mean-spirited and contemptible in every respect,*" even when the men became totally dependent on the food they were providing them with. Reluctantly relying on their generosity, Wills wrote: "*I suppose this will end in our having to live like the blacks for a few months.*"

Lord Alderdice, a Liberal Democrat member of UK's House of Lords, and a descendant of the expedition's sole survivor, John King, says that in contrast with King, who respected the Aborigines' knowledge of the land, Burke was very dismissive of them.[60] Burke fired his gun over the head of a man who'd brought him some food and asked for a piece of cloth in return.

Later it was reported that Burke rudely refused an offer of fish. After a while, the Yandruwandha stopped bringing the men food and eventually moved on. Without their benefactors, the explorers struggled to locate the nardoo seed, an aquatic fern that the Aborigines used to make cakes. This was because they were looking in the wrong places – they'd wrongly assumed that the seeds were growing on trees. Once they found the seeds, the explorers ate them green, not knowing that the nardoo seed is toxic if it is not correctly prepared (it drains the body of vitamin B1, which leads to death from malnutrition).

As a result of malnutrition, Burke ended up being unable to move, on the bank of the Cooper River. He asked King to place a pistol in his hand and to leave him unburied. He died later that day. King searched in vain for the Yandruwandha, and when he returned to camp, he found that Wills had died. After he had buried him, King set out again to look for the Yandruwandha, finally locating them. Lord Alderdice points out that the only reason King survived was due to his interest in the Aboriginal people and his respect for their knowledge of the land. King lived with the Yandruwandha for more than two months until a relief party sent from Melbourne discovered him on 15 September 1861.

The great irony is that Burke and Wills showed incredible fortitude and courage in being the first white people to cross the Australian continent. They perished because they didn't open themselves up to an unknown and untrusted source of knowledge. They failed to learn from the inhabitants of the unknown; being unable to conceive that these inhabitants possessed more knowledge than they did. They didn't trust them. Had their attitude towards new knowledge from the unknown been different, they would have survived.

Throughout the ages many people from different disciplines have tried to make sense of the unknown. There are stories worldwide of situations where Not Knowing is accepted, even embraced, and seen as a key driver of success. Not Knowing is central to many domains, from creativity in art to behavioural change in psychotherapy, new discoveries in science, exploring new frontiers in adventuring and creating new value in entrepreneurship. The way people operating in these domains use Not Knowing as a source of creativity and possibility is instructive for those of us struggling to learn about it.

Let's not "do a Burke and Wills." Let's keep our minds open and explore these diverse experiences and perspectives. No matter whether we've already travelled in the unknown or this is our first time, let's learn from the inhabitants of this place – the *"poets and inventors of fables,"* as Plutarch describes them. In this next section we meet some of them.

3.
THE ARTIST – THE SPACE BETWEEN ANGELS AND DEMONS

"We deserve our birthright, which is the middle way, an open state of mind that can relax with paradox and ambiguity."

Pema Chödrön

Artists are at home at the edge. They inhabit the creative space of in-between. This space appears to open after what has been described as the destruction of the ego.

Marshall Arisman, an American painter, illustrator, storyteller and educator, born in 1937, has been featured widely in the press from *TIME* magazine to *Mother Jones*. Permanent collections of his work are displayed in the Smithsonian and the Museum of American Art. One of his most famous images is the iconic cover of the novel *American Psycho* by Bret Easton Ellis, portraying the protagonist, Patrick Bateman, as part-man, part-devil.

Marshall confides that his creative process has stayed the same for nearly 50 years. He gets up in the morning, gets dressed and goes to his studio. *"What takes me there is my ego. I am in front of a blank canvas, thinking 'I'll do the best painting I have ever done'. What I forget is that my ego can't paint but it does get me to the studio! In front of the blank canvas my ego doesn't know what to do, so I start painting."*

The process of creating a painting always starts with something, normally a photo. He puts it up and thinks "I'll paint this frog." In the middle of the process, though, if the frog looks like a pig, he lets it be that. He never knows where he is going. In fact, he thinks that his best paintings are those where he is trying to control things less.

"Twenty minutes later I realize my painting is not so good. I start to argue with myself: 'this is not good', 'you should stop now and give up', 'you never could paint'." This internal argument goes on for 20 minutes, sometimes for up to two hours, until he acknowledges "this is still terrible!"

Marshall explains that it is at this point that his ego starts to recede a little. *"Somewhere in the middle of this destruction is the part of me that can paint and it energizes only when I've decided that what I've done from ego is worthless. There is a little space. It does not last long, 15 minutes perhaps, but it's enough. I can only get to this space through the destruction of my ego."*

For Marshall what is created through this process does not come from him, but "through" him. *"When people say to me 'I love your paintings', I reply 'I wasn't there'. Mark Rothko also alluded to the fact that he was a channel. Energy came through him. I cherish this space. I'm addicted to it. Now being 75 years old, my ego is not attached to painting, but to finding the space again. But never am I able to stay there."*

Letting go of the ego is a key part of the programme Marshall teaches at the School for Visual Arts in New York. He first asks his students to stand up and tell their story, which must be true, with pictures. At the beginning they are extremely self-conscious, telling it in a way that is unnatural, feeling shy standing in front of the group. Then he gets them to retell the story for two to three weeks, culminating in retelling it with a dog-mask on. Eventually the students are able to let go of their ego and relive the moment as they tell the story. *"They are closer to it,"* he says. *"At that point we get good stories."*

Marshall recalls his grandmother, who was a noted psychic and spiritualist. *"She lived in a community of mediums and I spent much of my childhood surrounded by psychics. She said to me 'You must learn in your life to stand in the space between angels and demons. Angels are playfully seductive and tempting, demons are interesting and dangerous'. In my study now I literally work in that middle space. I have paintings of angels on one side of the wall and demons on the other. I think this Not Knowing space is the 'human' space of being in between."*

ADVENTURING INTO THE UNKNOWN

4.

THE EXPLORER
– ONE MOUNTAIN AT A TIME

"It is not the mountain we conquer,
but ourselves."

Mountaineer Sir Edmund Hillary

Edurne Pasaban was the first woman to climb all fourteen 8,000m mountains in the world. Her experiences provide powerful insights into the challenges we all face when we venture into uncharted territory.

Edurne grew up in a small picturesque town called Tolosa in the Spanish Basque country. As a teenager she fell in love with the mountains, reaching her first summit, Mont Blanc, when she was 15 years old. By the time she reached 16, she had climbed seven peaks in the Andes, including Ecuador's Mount Chimborazo, 6,310m high.

"At this age, while all the other girls would be interested in spending their holidays with the boys, my heart was in climbing. I was a member of a small team of more experienced climbers. They were patient with me and taught me a lot. This early mentoring was important and helped give me confidence."

In 2001 she reached the Everest summit in her first expedition to the Himalaya. It was on her return that her father gave her an ultimatum: choose the family business or commit to climbing, as she could not do both. So she chose mountaineering.

After scaling Everest, Edurne began to climb one or two 8,000m mountains each year. Importantly, when she began this mission, she could not conceive of being able to climb all of them.

"Each took so much energy and commitment, it would have been crazy for me to even entertain that thought. It was only after I had completed my ninth 8,000'er that I thought that it may be possible to do them all, because I could see the end." In contrast to popular approaches to achievement, Edurne did not start with the "end in mind." She just started climbing and kept on climbing. The final achievement became clear as she progressed.

Edurne's climbing journey has not been easy. In 2004 she reached the summit of K2, considered the world's most dangerous mountain, but she lost two toes to frostbite and almost lost her life. She descended safely with the help of her team and Sherpas, who brought oxygen. She is certain that if it weren't for them, she wouldn't be here today. For explorers, surviving in the unknown is only possible with the support of others.

Losing her toes was not the most difficult period of Edurne's life, though. That happened off the mountain. *"When I came home I was 32 and all my friends were married and had different lives from me. I asked many questions of myself – what I was doing with my life, whether I should continue climbing and travelling into the unknown, or have a normal life and motherhood... I had a lasting depression and for four months I stayed in hospital not feeling well, thinking I did not like my life."*

Edurne's family, friends and climbing team helped her through this period. They reminded her about when she was at her happiest – climbing mountains or at a base camp.

"They helped reassure me that although I had a different life to them, I was happy in my own one. They encouraged me to try again. So after one year I organized another expedition and I committed to completing all 14 mountains. The most difficult moment in the unknown is to lose motivation to continue, so when you have people who understand you, they make your life easier."

It is the climber's ability to listen closely to the body and heart, rather than just the head. In 2001 Edurne was only 200m from the summit of a mountain with an Italian team. She had a very bad feeling that would not go away – she could not name it, but she didn't feel well. Even though she was close to reaching the peak, she chose to listen to her intuition and made the very difficult decision to go back down. She passed two Spanish colleagues on the way down who tried to persuade her to go back up with them. As she had paid a lot of attention to how she was feeling and had made up her mind, she refused. She later found out that one of the Spanish climbers had lost their life exactly in the area she'd had a bad feeling about. *"When your intuition speaks, you need to listen,"* Edurne advises.

Edurne believes that when venturing into the unknown celebrating milestones and little successes along the way is very important – even if the end result might be years away. *"Identify those significant moments; they are important steps. Make sure you don't diminish your achievements. Celebrate with those who have helped you get there. I believe that we all have one life. Nobody can give me a second one."*

5.

THE PSYCHOTHERAPIST
– THE WAY OF UNKNOWING

"Discard your memory; discard the future tense of our desire; forget them both, both what you knew and what you want, to leave space for a new idea."

Psychoanalyst Wilfred Bion

There is a rich tradition in Western theology and philosophy that speaks of Not Knowing as "the way of unknowing." This concept features prominently in the dialogue between psychotherapy and spirituality. For Dr Peter Tyler, reader in pastoral theology and spirituality and senior lecturer in theology at St Mary's University, Twickenham, London, this concept directly influences his pastoral work as an integrative psychotherapist.

Peter quotes Austrian philosopher Ludwig Wittgenstein who said that our language is always referring to that which is beyond language but cannot grasp. *"Language and discourse, suggests Wittgenstein, is a choreography between what is said and what is not said, or rather, what is said and what is shown. Our intellects can grasp only one half of the equation. For full reality to be present both the known and the unknown – the said and the shown – must be present."*

Nowhere is this better illustrated for Peter than in his work as a psychotherapist. Whenever a client comes into the room, he faces a choice: either rely on his learning and training, or try to enter into a place of unknowing with the client. This approach is in line with Wilfred Bion, the British psychoanalyst, who describes this challenge:

"When we are in the office with a patient we have to dare to rest. It is difficult to see what is at all frightening about that, but it is. It is difficult to remain quiet and let the patient have a chance to say whatever he or she has to say. It is frightening for the patient – and the patient hates it. We are under constant pressure to say something, to admit that we are doctors or psychoanalysts or social workers, to supply some box into which we can be put complete with a label."[61]

Peter heeds Bion's advice for psychotherapists to discard memory and desire and have the courage and humility to step into a "space of unknowing." This is a place that requires memories, the need to control, and "*all the whirring chatter of the 'monkey mind*'" to be put aside, to be present for others. For Peter this means listening to the present moment and to what that person is bringing to the encounter in the here and now. As he explains, this can sometimes take a surprising turn:

"The surprise can come in an idea, picture or even tune that comes to mind, or physically in a sensation or emotion that arises. Before the session begins I always do a quick self-scan or self-check of where I am emotionally, physically and psychologically. In nine times out of 10, when a new or surprising feeling, thought, physical sensation or emotion occurs during the session, I can be pretty sure it has been influenced by the presence of the other before me. This may take the form of a tightening in the head or shoulders, a sense of anger, fear or lethargy, even a picture or striking memory that has not occurred to me for some time."

Peter recognizes this as what psychologists call "transference and counter-transference." By practising the presence of un-knowing these sensations, feelings and thoughts can be thrown into greater relief so that the therapist is in a better position to isolate them and work with them in a more conscious way with the client. *"I must say that after nearly 20 years of practice, this is one area where experience comes to our aid."*

According to Peter, the path of unknowing is not equivalent to ignorance. In medieval times it was called the way of "stulta sapientia," literally "learned ignorance" or "foolish wisdom": we must train in the skills of our profession, whether we are a business manager, doctor, nurse, psychoanalyst or teacher, but we must learn to know when to keep silent – when to let the demands of the ego quieten and the unknown element of show-ing reveal itself. Peter says that this art of when to speak and when to keep silent makes the difference in our interpersonal encounters. *"In a world saturated with information, false 'know-ing' and the blinkered opinions of 'specialists', I would suggest the time for 'learned ignorance' has returned... no more so than in the highly stressed and driven worlds of commerce, transaction and business."*

6.
THE SCIENTIST
– FREEDOM TO DEVIATE

"Being a scientist requires having faith in uncertainty, finding pleasure in mystery, and learning to cultivate doubt. There is no surer way to screw up an experiment than to be certain of its outcome."

Neuroscientist Stuart Firestein

One of the most direct ways of engaging with the unknown is the open inquiry and experimental methodology of the scientific method. Not Knowing plays a vital role in how hypotheses are formulated, experiments conducted and new discoveries made. Hans Hoppe, a senior bio-scientist at the University of Oxford, reflects on the part that Not Knowing plays in the scientific process.

"It was a Tuesday afternoon in the autumn of 2010 when I realized that the data staring back at me from my computer screen was telling me something annoying: still nothing. There was no way for me, given current thinking in my field, to understand what I had been looking at for several weeks."

Hans had gone through all possible permutations of the prevailing theory that he could think of, trying to explain the data in front of him. He wanted to bring the data into the context of current understanding of how proteins can improve their function, but none of his assumptions made any sense. Hans was researching the reason for the appearance of a completely new function in a cell-surface receptor, a function that arose very suddenly during evolution. As this was an unusual change, Hans was perplexed. He wondered what else could be behind the change and how a completely new function could evolve.

He could have ignored this aspect, left it as some observational data outside his area of expertise and moved on. But the molecule was too important and he was also too excited about having discovered something new and surprising to let it go. At this point in his work it had taken over five years and a team of 16 scientists from three continents to describe the findings. *"Yet I was still staring at the question of why and all I managed to achieve was to move from 'no answer yet' to 'no answer possible from within my field of protein science'. The situation was very frustrating."*

Hans describes this period as strangely exciting at the same time. While he found himself truly at the limits of his knowledge with his current knowledge and skills, aware of the unknown ahead, he also felt a sense of freedom to be able to explore something new. This mindset enabled Hans to change his frame of reference completely and eventually led to a significant discovery in his field. Reflecting on the process, Hans describes the role Not Knowing plays in science:

"Sometimes the most significant aspect of researching the unknown in science is realizing where it begins. Yet we do not normally think in this way. Instead, we concentrate on 'where our knowledge ends'. This is only natural, for after all it is only our detailed knowledge and experience which enables new observations. Mostly, this amounts to tackling the unknown in a 'filling in the blanks' approach to substantiate known theories."

He argues that when small steps in theory adjustment lead nowhere, leaps in our understanding are required, a phenomenon American physicist Thomas Kuhn termed "paradigm shift."

Hans points out that new insights require fresh thinking, which in turn requires a degree of freedom from certain constraints acting on the individual, both material and mental. He believes that mental constraints are more difficult to recognize and put aside, especially when they arise from the very knowledge that made the new observations possible in the first place. *"As with my evolution research mentioned earlier, it is often the realization that an extension to the chosen framework of knowledge will not yield a sufficient solution which frees the mind and enables the search for new concepts as the old ones are abandoned. A process which instils a sense of freedom, or a license to venture out."*

Hans argues that letting go of the known and opening up to ideas previously considered too strange to explore are individual decisions that play a fundamental part in the scientific process, beyond filling in the gaps. *"Once the newly expanded frame of knowledge is accepted and the boundaries of the unknown are drawn afresh, the cycle of 'filling in the gaps' research into the unknown can resume. At least, until another observation creates an obstacle to knowledge as we know it, sparking a new opportunity to let go of the known and to venture out."*

When science resembles knowledge acquisition, the freedom to deviate from a hypothesis can easily become seen as an unnecessary delay and distraction, reducing scientific research to a quest for usefulness. To advance real scientific progress beyond currently predictable applications, more consideration for individual freedom to think laterally, or "outside the box" is beneficial as it encourages personal ventures into the collectively unknown.

7.
THE ENTREPRENEUR
– DISCOVERING WHAT'S NEXT

"Not Knowing is what makes being an entrepreneur more amazing than working a regular desk job with a regular paycheck. We take risks, we fail, we don't know what's going to happen, we not only put our toes into the waters of the unknown ... we dive in, headfirst."

Author Leo Babauta

For Joseph Pistrui, Professor of Entrepreneurial Management at IE Business School in Madrid, Not Knowing is a way of engaging with the "now" to capitalize on the opportunities that it presents.

Joseph points out that as executives find themselves more and more in situations in which their own experience is not particularly useful, they need to adopt a novel approach. When operating in the unknown, they need to rely more on their ability to "sense" the circumstances laid before them, rather than "know" the circumstances based on past experience alone.

"Holding what you know and allowing that you do not know becomes a critically important framing in today's world of leading and managing." Joseph believes that this attitude enables executives to operate more effectively in the present and become more effective in identifying fresh opportunities.

Entrepreneurship is a way of addressing uncertainty and the unknown. *"I'm seeing a transition; a move from a business 'plan'-centred view of leading to a 'problem'-centred view of leading. Less energy is spent on the plan while more is focused on understanding the problem which may be unknown, maybe unknowable!"* For Joseph, entrepreneurship is a process of converting high uncertainty and unknowns, systematically, to the more known, through hard evidence. *"When that shift in mindset is embraced, the unknown can be liberating. Working this process with others promotes divergent thinking and allows for emergent questions, such as 'what could be?' The historical management approaches didn't exploit this capability,"* he explains.

Joseph finds Not Knowing empowering. He believes that when we don't have a concrete starting point, anything is possible. To this end he developed the concept of "Nextsensing,"a way for experienced executives to work with Not Knowing and become more comfortable engaging with the unknown. *"Most organizations have a quite well-articulated decision gate process but at the early stage of what designers call the 'fuzzy front end' – what I call 'disruptive ambiguity' – this can be overwhelming. And when executives are in this early stage, they need to socialize their ideas. The Nextsensing process is a systematic way executives can talk themselves forward by sharing insight and building a new sense of things."*

In his work Joseph has seen the many forms of disruption, from changing data patterns, serendipity, and things that are unexpected. He argues that the challenge at this point is not to accept the first ideas that come to mind as a given, but to test them as assumptions rather than take them as fact. He works with executives to detect change early by helping them better understand the situation "as it presents itself now." By deeply understanding the present, they are more likely to develop "presumptive hunches" that will give them insights they can use to work their way forwards.

He believes that it's the responsibility of everyone to participate in sensing what the future of an organization could be because insights can come from anywhere, at every level. *"Successful organizations and their teams will have to embrace and engage in Not Knowing to find their next competitive advantage."*

These diverse stories from art, science, adventuring, psychotherapy and entrepreneurship show that Not Knowing has a broad relevance, evidenced not only in history but also in everyday practice. Yet if we accept that there is value in Not Knowing, how are we to develop such a way of being in the world? We turn to this next.

PART III - "NEGATIVE" CAPABILITIES

On 21 December 1817, Keats wrote a letter to his brothers George and Thomas. He had been having a public disagreement with another great English poet, Coleridge. Keats felt that Coleridge was obsessed with seeking categorical knowledge and explanations for the mysteries of the natural world. Keats was intrigued about what state of mind is necessary for creative genius, particularly in literature. He described a special quality that he admired in Shakespeare, who, in contrast to Coleridge, he considered to be *"capable of being in uncertainties, Mysteries, doubts, without irritable reaching after fact & reason."*[62] He called this "negative capability." The people in the stories above embody this capability.

This idea of negative capability is powerful because it captures the need for making space in the mind to allow new thoughts to take root. It clears the mind of existing knowledge, clichés or existing assumptions. In addition, it captures the paradox that making space (negating what's already in the mind) is a capability. It is a skill, an ability that some people have, but which can also be fostered. It takes positive energy, focus and practice to develop the skill of negative capability – it doesn't just happen all by itself.

A century later, English academics Robert French and Peter Simpson brought the concept of negative capability into the business and leadership domains. They argue that only through combining positive capabilities, such as knowledge, skills and competencies, with negative capabilities, such as silence, patience, doubt and humility, can we create a space of learning and creativity at the edge.[63]

They argue that *"organizational leaders must be oriented towards the unknown, creative insight of the moment and hence towards 'the edges' of their ignorance"*[64] to *"establish or to*

maintain their competitive advantage and to ensure that their
organization can thrive in the face of competition and market
forces, or to make sure that the needs of clients are met."[65]

Although there are many lessons to be drawn from
diverse professions where Not Knowing is central to
success, how can we use Not Knowing in situations where
we are expected to know, or to make clear decisions?
What capabilities can be transposed in these more
"knowledge worshipping" areas, from corporate and
political leadership to social situations? In the sections
that follow we extract the essence from the professions
where Not Knowing is a requirement for success, and
apply it to the areas where Not Knowing is seen to
be a liability. These sections are oriented towards the
unknown. We have focused solely on the "negative"
capabilities needed to survive and flourish in the
unknown, as these are the ones that are usually
neglected in the world of work.

It would go against the spirit of this book, however, for
us to merely give you a map of how to engage with
the unknown. As soon as you had the map, you would
have to leave it on the cliff behind you anyway. Not
Knowing cannot be mapped; it is a state that can only be
experienced, and that experience will be unique to you.

We have written these sections in the spirit of
exploration and discovery. We hope that the ideas
might help awaken you to the possibility of Not Knowing,
so that it may be a helpful companion to you on your
journey. We have grouped the negative capabilities under
four different headings that we've called "empty your
cup," "close your eyes to see," "leap in the dark," and
"delight in the unknown."

EMPTY YOUR CUP

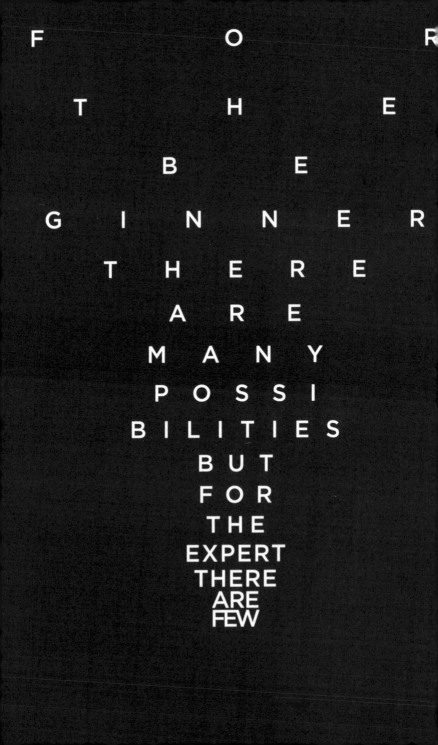

CHAPTER 6

1.

BEGINNER'S MIND

A young manager who was very confident in his abilities and who had been promoted to a Vice President role in his company within a year of joining, had an appointment with his Managing Director (MD). He wanted to find out from the MD what it took to rise to the next grade. He was very keen to be promoted again, and soon.

The MD welcomed him into his office and offered the young manager a cup of coffee. Quickly accepting, the young manager started to describe all his achievements and what he knew about the business. He wanted to impress. As the young manager offered his cup to be filled with coffee, the MD kept on pouring into the cup until it overflowed and started spilling onto the carpet.

Startled, the young manager asked: *"What are you doing? Why do you keep on pouring when my cup is already full?"* The MD replied: *"It is because your cup is already full that you are learning nothing from this meeting."*

Not Knowing is emphasized in Zen practice where it is sometimes called "beginner's mind." An expert may think they know a subject deeply, yet be blinded to new possibilities by his or her preconceived ideas. In contrast, a beginner may see with fresh, unbiased eyes. The practice of beginner's mind is to cultivate an ability to meet life without holding on to preconceived ideas, interpretations or judgements.

When we are full of our own thoughts we have no ability to take on new learning and respond to reality as it presents itself in the actual moment. It is not about getting rid of our experience and wisdom, but rather not letting it get in the way of seeing things from a fresh perspective.

The more successful we are, the more tempting it is to believe that we already know what to do. Every project, every problem is different, so approaching a new challenge as if we've seen it all before, and applying already known and tested solutions, can lead to making errors. For example, some large consulting firms are sometimes perceived as making any problem fit their existing model. This is cost-effective because the firm will have already invested time developing its proprietary process that can be scaled and applied to many diverse client problems. A colleague remembers once meeting a very senior manager who was renowned in corporate America. He spent a lot of time telling her how interesting his life was and then he said: *"You know, I've seen it all. I've had a long career and there isn't any issue that I have not been through before."* She was shocked by his arrogance. *"It was clearly nonsense that he had seen it all. Even if he had been involved in 100 mergers, the 101st was not simply a cut and paste of one of the previous 99."*

At the One Young World Summit in 2012, Mohammad Yunnus spoke about the way he started the Grameen Bank. Grameen is now a Nobel Peace Prize-winning microfinance organization and community development bank. Yunnus said that the best thing that happened to him was that he didn't know anything about banking. In fact, if he'd known anything about banking he wouldn't have embarked on the micro-credit project in the first place.[66] *"Not knowing something can be a blessing sometimes. You are open, you can do things in your way without worrying about the rules and procedures. [...] Every time I needed a rule or a procedure I had to look at what conventional banks do, and once I learned what they did, I did the opposite. Conventional banks go to the rich, I go to the poor. Conventional banks go to men, I go to the women. Conventional banks are owned by rich people, Grameen Bank is owned by poor people. **I could try because I didn't know anything.**"* His advice to young entrepreneurs is: *"Don't be scared if you don't know something, don't feel you have to be very smart to do something, stupid people like us do something and it works out."*[67]

According to Dr Christian Busch PhD, Associate Director at the London School of Economics Innovation Lab and Co-Founder of the Sandbox Network, modern micro-credit, mobile banking and micro-saving are all intriguing innovations that have come out of contexts where there was no real infrastructure in place before. So there was no need to institutionally unlearn; there was no pre-existing conception of "how things are done." For Christian these examples illustrate how a "don't know mindset" can trigger innovation without the baggage of history or existing path dependencies.

Christian points out that many interesting recent innovations have come out of resource-constrained environments, where there might either not be a pre-conception of a product/ service/ business model, or where the pre-conception is so far out of reach (e.g. cost-wise) that it is only peripherally taken into account. He gives the example of mobile banking in Kenya, where the process of people transferring airtime to their friends and families established an alternative to traditional banking services.

"In a country where banks are either difficult to access or rarely affordable, one does not necessarily limit one's thinking to how to design a better cash machine. Rather, the challenge is tackled from a different angle: 1) We have mobile phones; 2) We have value that needs to be transferred (first airtime, then money); 3) We establish a platform for money-transactions that makes many of the institutionalized banking practices redundant. Whether 'not knowing' or 'not having access to', these innovations come out of environments where pre-conditions (such as institutions) are either not available, or not accessible."

Radisson Blu Hotels (formerly Radisson Edwardian) in the UK during the 1990s made the then radical decision to take their

General Managers out of their hotels and make them responsible for different areas across the hotel chain, such as food and beverages or room service. Every two or three years they would get the opportunity to change their expert domains and become a beginner again. This way they could apply their knowledge to a new area in the business while bringing fresh perspectives and looking for interconnections between seemingly separate disciplines.

It is said that Morihei Ueshiba, the founder of the martial art Aikido, asked before he died at the age of 85 that he be buried wearing a white belt, the lowest in the belt rankings. Similarly, the most senior Aikido Masters choose to teach the basics of Aikido, a conscious choice to inhabit the "beginner" space. We too can make beginner's mind a conscious choice and open up the space for new learning and growth.

Don't Know mindset

"Don't Know mindset" is a central concept in the Eastern traditions. It simply means not prejudging a situation. In martial arts it means not assuming we will lose or win on the basis of knowing our opponent. Whether they seem stronger or weaker than us, we acknowledge that our judgement may be wrong, so we suspend it and keep an open mind. "Anything can happen" is a much better position to be in than expecting that we will win, then finding ourselves thrown on the mat.

In terms of competitive strategy, just because an organization looks weaker or smaller or seems to have worse products, we can't prejudge who will win in a competitive market. With this lens, we need to have a strategy that allows for the competitor to be in a winning position as well as a weaker position vis-à-vis our organization. People in business are much more likely to be comfortable relying on analysis that tells them whether a competitor is likely to win or not. However, the "don't know mindset," or we could call it "don't know strategy," admits the possibility of winning or losing at the same time. This approach prepares for both possibilities and manages the benefits and risks of both. It doesn't close off the possibility that the competitor could beat or even destroy the company's business. Also it acknowledges that our competitor may not even be on our radar. For example, 10 years ago we may not have predicted that supermarkets would be competitors to banks, providing personal finance products.

NEW LEARNING

2.

FROM CONTROL TO TRUST

"Trust people and they will be true to you; treat them greatly and they will show themselves great."

American author Ralph Waldo Emerson

What happens if you throw out the organizational chart, take away roles and responsibilities, let people decide on their own salaries, working hours and holidays? What happens if you create the space for trust rather than control? This is exactly what Peter King did as the general manager of Energeticos, an engineering company in the South American country of Colombia, part of the Scotland-based Wood Group. The firm was making a loss in 2004, but by 2012 had grown from 60 to 1,050 people with annual sales growing from $4m to $56m USD. Not only had it become financially profitable, but the workforce was alive with energy.

A key part of the success of the transformation was moving away from control from the top down to allowing leadership and decisions to take place within the workforce itself. It involved letting go of the belief that people cannot be trusted and instead trusting that people have a genuine intrinsic motivation to do good work if they are given autonomy, purpose and responsibility.

Peter took on the role of GM for Energeticos in June 2003, a new role for him. He recalls: *"I remember walking into the office scared stiff but I knew that this was normal and it would take time before I felt comfortable."*

When Peter arrived at Energeticos it was barely making a profit and in 2004 it made a loss of $300,000 USD. For a small company of only 60 employees, this was a lot to lose. The firm was bailed out by a sister company of the Wood Group which gave it a lifeline. Peter decided that it would no longer be enough simply to bump along. The situation needed to change radically. At the time he had read a book called *Maverick* by Brazilian CEO Ricardo Semler on how he had transformed his company by doing radical things to empower his employees. When he read it he felt "this is what companies should be like." Companies should be built on trust.

"Rising early, I went into the office at 6.45 and started writing my own company 'manual'. I continued writing till 9am and was finished. It was only a little manual, 5" x 3" a few pages, not a long tome. With both nervousness and excitement I sent the booklet out to staff. I did this without permission from Head Office."

Central to the changes he instigated at Energeticos was Peter's belief that people work better with trust and a sense of responsibility. *"I remember having a secretary in Aberdeen, Scotland, who typed a letter for me and gave it to me to sign. I said 'thanks' and signed it, without looking at it. She was stunned and asked 'Aren't you going to read it?' 'No,' I said. Later she came back with another letter and again I signed it without reading. If you are not watching people, and they know you are not watching them, they are more conscious of doing the job properly."*

Energeticos started publishing everything for staff, even management salaries. This surprised people for a while, and then it just became the norm. Peter also gave the responsibility to the staff to decide on what their own salaries should be. There were

70 process engineers at the time in 2011, who were all upset about their salaries. They were all told what was in the budget, the financial situation of the company with complete transparency, and the comparative salary benchmark for their role with Energeticos' competitors. Peter asked them to organize themselves and come up with their own level grading schemes and salaries. They did exactly that. It was very hard work and involved time for them to work it through, but they came back with a good grading system and salaries that were highly competitive.

Peter reflects: *"When I asked people to take responsibility I also promised that I would go with whatever they came up with. Even if I disagreed or thought it was silly. It was important to keep my promise and show real trust. They never came up with something stupid when we told them the truth. These occasions gave me a lot of confidence in human beings. When we are given trust and responsibility, overwhelmingly we do our best."*

The experienced engineers who were in their 50s and 60s played a key role in mentoring the younger staff in sharing their experience at Energeticos. They were much loved and groups of young engineers would go to them for support and advice. They even created an Energeticos School to share ideas and experience from 7-9am. No additional pay was involved; it was simply established for the sheer zest for learning. It took three months for management to even know it was happening, when a poster was noticed on a wall. Peter recalls this as being a very satisfying moment, to see how they could organize themselves without the push from top-down leadership.

Peter also did away with the established hierarchy. The organization functioned in teams allocated for projects and leaders allocated to various disciplines. Energeticos didn't even have an organizational chart; it was simply not needed anymore. People found other, more creative ways to organize themselves. He explains how he created the space for staff to find their own role, one that they were suited for, rather than given to them through a job description:

"Roles and responsibilities only become important when you have them. When we found good people who applied to the company we would give them three months to wander around the company and then tell us what they would like to do. Lots of companies want to label and assign a role to people too early. One person ended up on the commercial side, another became a project engineering supervisor and one came as a document controller and ended up as an IT manager. Two ladies serving coffee ended up in purchasing. We looked at the person, not the role, and were flexible."

Having a trust-based culture did not mean there were no difficult decisions to be made. At one point the company was not bringing in enough income and needed to let go of staff. *"We stayed with our principles and got managers to sit with groups of 10 staff to share with them openly the company situation. All staff understood what we were doing and appreciated us giving them time of two to three weeks to search for other opportunities rather than telling them on a Friday afternoon that they had lost their job. Those that left went on the First Back list. We treated people with respect as a partner in the business."*

"Not Knowing is considering that there are other ways of working and doing things. A lot of people explore new ideas. Mine was not a tentative exploration. I was passionate about this," says Peter. This philosophy is characteristic of his leadership approach.

Peter helped the people at Energeticos manage the disequilibrium created by the change by giving them the freedom to make decisions and empowering them to take responsibility for the business. His willingness to give up control and instead trust in people's abilities created a culture that enabled people to face up to their own challenges, rather than revert to relying on those higher up to solve them.

Vlatka Hlupic, Professor of Business and Management at West-minster Business School in London, specializes in studying organizations that move away from traditional, command and control approaches to collaborative approaches.[68] She has found that when employees are given the freedom to self-organize in groups according to their own interests and experiment with new ideas, they are not only more engaged and motivated to perform, but there is also a significant positive impact on the organization's bottom line. Paradoxically, giving up control and power creates the conditions for increased power, because more things get done and more can be achieved.

A useful idea in Peter's story is the concept of "pacing." He did not relinquish total control, something which may have left the employees feeling too much uncertainty. Instead he was able to transition from control to trust gradually, allowing people to adapt to having more responsibility.

Our ability to engage with Not Knowing is related to our willing-ness to let go of control and engage with what is. Our challenge is to value our powerlessness as much as our expertise. This comes not from a place of nihilism, but from a place of humil-ity; to see the possibility that is only available by acknowledging the limits of our expertise and going beyond the edges of what we know.

CONTRUST

3.

HOLD ON TO PURPOSE AND VALUES

"He who has a why to live for can bear almost any how."

Philosopher Friedrich Nietzsche

One day CEO and founder of architectural and engineering company AE Works, Michael Cherock, came across a shocking discovery – his company was close to collapse. What made it worse was that nobody knew what was happening, even those he had hired to have senior accountability.

"Everything stopped on June 4, 2012. Being the first Monday of the month, it was reserved for financial activities like billing. AE Works, the company I founded in my basement five years before, was a growing firm and I was proud of what we had accomplished.

At 9am, as I settled in our cramped conference room and started to review our financials for the month, a very unsettled feeling started to come over me. My growing concern and mounting questions were halted with the start of the next scheduled appointment, an important meeting to finalize financing for a new office that we were moving into, only two months away.

"Concluding that meeting, I returned to the papers. The new debt I had just created to finance our new office still haunted me. Desperate for answers, I turned to the papers that would tell the story of our billings. I flipped to the final total and lowered my head in despair. What I had been feeling, but hoped wasn't true, was quickly becoming my reality. My company was grossly out of balance."

Starting to comprehend the company's perilous financial situation, Michael turned to his inner circle, the firm's operations manager, Senior Vice President (SVP) and accountant, all of whom he had known for years. Each individual possessed a great professional reputation, had accrued decades of experience and insight into the inner workings of the industry. Michael trusted them and believed they shared a common vision for the future.

Searching for clarity, Michael first started questioning the firm's Operations Manager. He didn't seem to know why the company was in such a situation, and worse, he didn't see that there was any reason for concern. Anxiety increasing, Michael then called the most senior man in the company besides himself, the SVP and head of sales. As he explained the situation, Michael realized that the SVP knew little of what had been produced on the operations side of the business. He could hear the growing concern in his voice as the conversation revealed that the firm was producing fewer billings and increasing liabilities through spending more on new opportunities. Securing new hires and resources to perform new work was expansive but costly. This abysmal trajectory meant only one thing – the firm was quickly moving into a position where it would not be able to meet its obligations.

"Only one more call stood between me and what now seemed impending failure. As I divulged the situation to my accountant, he told me that based on a quick analysis, the firm, which up to this point appeared stronger than ever, was on the brink of financial

collapse. I couldn't believe what I was hearing. How did this come to be? As I probed his understanding of our business, I quickly came to realize that he knew little of the details in the transactions. My mounting stress became anger. My company took a hit and no one knew why. The people I had paid and entrusted the company to had not done their job. I was mad as hell. That's when everything I had believed came crashing down around me."

The clock read 5pm. Still in the same conference room where the day's events were set in motion, Michael sat in silence. For the first time, the company he had started five years prior was in danger of going under.

"All my hard work, long hours, and financial risk could result in nothing but failure. The increasing probability of this outcome brought tears to my eyes. The hope felt by family, friends, clients, and staff – all those people who believed in me and joined me to create something new – would now be lost due to bad management. Thoughts of their collective disappointment made me feel sick. Of all those thoughts, what devastated me most was that it seemed that I had no idea what was happening in the company."

Michael felt exposed and more vulnerable than he had ever been. In his greatest moment of despair, he found overwhelming confidence in his purpose and his values. These values had guided his decision-making over a lifetime, and had led to the creation of a company in which they would be shared in the lives of others. He realized how little he knew at that moment, but the clarity of his values gave him a feeling of security. After all, people had taken a big risk to join his fledgling business because of those shared values. He believed that the shared belief system was in fact their greatest potential.

"These values would gain more meaning in our work as we learned to share our vulnerabilities and trust one another to create opportunities and turn the company around. June 4, 2012 wouldn't mark our disaster. It would be the greatest learning opportunity

ever presented! With new work coming in, a new office to support our work and shared values, we could fix the mess I created."

Over the following months, Michael worked relentlessly to bring clarity to the vision and the collective belief system. Decisions became harder to take. He had to end relationships and incorporate considerable changes into the old structure and systems.

"Today, the company is built upon a culture that prizes open communication as our number-one asset. This builds trust in each other and our team. Championed by our value-based decision-making, this culture has allowed us to enjoy strong performances, both financial and creative. The reason for these successes? It's simple – the strength of our firm relies on our people and the strength of our connections to one another."

AE Works has since been recognized as a Pittsburgh 100 firm for two years running, and as an Inc. 5,000 honoree, one of the fastest growing companies in the US.

Purpose and values lie at the centre of our being. They give our lives meaning; they give us joy. In the depth of the unknown, clear values and purpose may be the only things that we can hold on to. They can be the compasses that help us orient and move forward even if we are unsure of the destination. Bill George who teaches "Authentic Leadership" at the Harvard Business School argues that our values help us find our "True North." They can hold us steady when the winds of change toss us around. Even if we may not know where we are heading, we know why.

4.
LET GO

"By holding on,
we destroy what we hope to preserve;
by letting go,
we feel secure in accepting what is."

Leadership author Margaret Wheatley

A photograph by artist Yves Klein, *Leap Into the Void*, is an iconic image of taking a leap into what seems like certain injury, into a street several feet below. Yet Klein's figure has a smile on his face. The artist was a trained martial artist and knew how to fall without incurring injury. The image of jumping into a liminal space is evocative. It is a powerful metaphor for leaving the security of the "ground," and for a time experiencing "groundlessness." Being in a space in which there is no certainty can also be a place of possibility, where different choices can be made. It can be a place of transformation. Imagine the skilled gymnast who seems to hover in space. She can choose any range of possible moves before coming back to land on her feet.

Steven: I wanted to experience what it was like to do my own 'leap into the void' and experience groundlessness. To do that I enrolled in a "Flying Trapeze" class in Regents Park, London. Since a child I have been scared of heights, so arriving at the class and seeing half a dozen people, some beginners like me, who would jump for the first time, seemed much more than theory. We were given the ground rules for safety. Although they sounded simple, they reminded me of what is needed to enter into the unknown. It is not a case of blindly following rules but finding what would best help support.

Rather than going straight to the 40ft trapeze, I started by practising on a trapeze that was only a few feet from the ground. I learnt to lift my body, raise my knees over the bar to hang and then again lower my feet and come back to the ground. I was then strapped up and began the climb up the ladder to do the jump. What struck me was that whilst I felt terrified, there were three school children, perhaps 11 years old, who were joking, seemingly at ease with the situation. I could see how seriously I was taking the activity and yet if I had the attitude of these younger boys I could have seen the challenge as play. Climbing up and being strapped in with safety ropes, I felt a trembling in my body, slight vertigo and nausea, but also excitement. Standing at the top, I thought I've committed myself now and there's no way back.

The call to jump came quicker than expected. How I would have wanted to jump on my own terms. Yet often we are called to jump before we are ready and we leap. As I leapt off the board there was a free-falling experience and then complete exhilaration as I flew through the air. All of the weight of my body was in my hands as I held on to the trapeze bar. At the top of the arc there is a place of least gravity and this is the time when it is best to lift the legs and hook them over the bar. I hooked my legs over. Not with ease, but I let gravity pull me backwards, lifting my hands off the bar and hanging from my knees. I was completely pulled by the movement with no effort on my part. This for me represented complete letting go and going with the movement rather than fighting it. It was the most exhilarating moment of the whole experience. I then raised my hands again and tried to descend gracefully with a back flip as instructed. That didn't happen! I fell to the safety of a mat below.

> *Jumping into the unknown is a practice. The jumpers who had done it before were better the second time and improved. I noticed my fear kick in and my fixed mindset that I'm just not good at this new skill. I've tried it once, but did not want to do it again. I believe this is my real challenge. Not to jump once, but to do so again and again till I can use that moment of space in a creative way.*

As we have seen in previous chapters, organizations and teams have expectations of the people in charge. This is hard-wired into us. When we find ourselves at the edge, unsure and confused, we are in danger of reverting to a dependent relationship with those in authority. We look to them to take responsibility away from us, to sort things out, to protect us. When our usual ways are no longer enough, when we haven't been here before, we don't readily tolerate people in authority Not Knowing.

When we move beyond our competence and approach the edge, we need to renegotiate the expectations that people may have on us. Peter King from Energeticos created a culture where staff relied on each other to set goals and stay accountable to those goals. By acknowledging that he didn't have all the answers, he left space for staff to develop their own approaches and to make their own decisions.

In spite of the risks, providing less direction allows for more learning and creativity. A study carried out in 2009 by scientists from the University of Louisville and MIT's Department of Brain and Cognitive Sciences took 48 children between the ages of three and six and presented them with a toy that had a variety of functions. Among other functions it could squeak, play notes, and reflect images. To one set of children only a single attribute was shown before they were allowed to play with the toy. For the other, no information was given about the toy. This group ended up playing for longer and discovering an average of six attributes of the toy, compared with the group that was told what to do, who discovered only four. A similar study at UC Berkeley demonstrated that kids given no instruction were much more likely to come up with novel solutions to a problem. Alison Gopnik, professor of psychology at UC Berkeley, argues that if you programme a robot with instructions, when the unexpected occurs it will freeze. But if you give it many options and then encourage it to learn from mistakes, it can meet fresh challenges.[69]

The challenge of leadership is to deliberately dissolve the illusion of knowledge and control that traditionally surrounds those in charge. When we can't solve our challenges alone, we need to engage and mobilize others, to help tackle the issues together.

So rather than taking up a predictable role of showing the way, jumping in to answer a question or solve a problem, we can try something different. When we are silent, we allow others to come in and perhaps take control. If we share our point of view after everyone has spoken, there may be more room for creativity. When we don't indicate what we think or prefer to happen, we create the space for a different conversation.

Over the past 15 years Beth Jandernoa, an organizational learning consultant with the Presencing Institute in Cambridge, Massachusetts, has seen many organizational change projects not go according to plan. She is an expert in the process involved in letting go.

One particular project stands out for her. It involved a global technology company that had been the industry leader for decades, but was losing its competitive edge. New nimble competitors were eating away at their market share. The company was desperate for innovative ideas, looking for a dramatic shift from "business as usual." Everyone in the organization shared a commitment to shift to a new way of operating. The executives took a risk; they opened their usually closed strategic planning process to involve 130 people in giving input and making decisions about where the division would go and how it would get there. It was the first time in the history of the company that suppliers, customers, and employees all along the value chain had participated in planning the future of the North American distribution. The executives had promised employees that their input would shape and influence the future design of the work processes, how the organization would then relate to customers and suppliers, and how decisions would be made.

It was a couple of days before the last conference, in which collective agreements on the strategy would be made. Four weeks had passed since the prior conference and Beth was on a call with her team to finalize the design. However, in their check-in the client representatives related some shocking news. Two weeks after the second conference, the executives received an ultimatum from the company's senior executive team to make some critical decisions earlier than had been expected. This meant jumping ahead of the timeline agreed upon with the employees, and making important decisions without the final input of the strategic planning participants. The representatives relayed the fact that rumors were flying around and that many employees were outraged, since they perceived this move to be a betrayal of the promise to include them in the process.

"I hadn't seen this coming and in the moment I could taste the fear of failure and imagine scenes of angry employees. In this place of Not Knowing I realized that I had to hold steady and to draw on skills and resources that I hadn't used before. As a team we knew we had to 'pull a rabbit out of a hat'; in other words, we had to find a path that would take us into new territory. We had to let go of our design and create a process to confront the perceived betrayal in a way that would re-build trust and commitment."

The team virtually stepped back, erased the agenda and began to design a way for employees and management to step into each other's shoes and to understand why management had taken the steps that they had and to hear the interpretation that the employees had made. Suddenly all the creative juices started to flow. They ordered two tall ladders to use in the conference: one for a manager to climb while answering questions, representing the story of management, and the second for an employee to climb while representing employees' reactions.

When the conference opened you could feel the tension in the room. But, instead of avoiding it, the team invited a manager and employee to come to the front of the room to represent the feelings and thoughts of each group. The room fell silent as the manager began to share her story of the urgency and pressure management was feeling and then the union employee revealed his view of the incident. As the manager and employee took each step up the ladder as they answered questions about what assumptions had driven their actions, what conclusions they had drawn, and what beliefs they were operating from, members of the audience, managers and employees alike, participated by calling out their answers to the questions as the two representatives climbed each step.

What became apparent to everyone were the good intentions displayed by each side and the misunderstandings that had driven people's actions. Once this was revealed, the mood of the whole group changed palpably. Trust that had become frayed was renewed and deepened, and the division went on to generate new pathways informed by this seeming disruption.

"My team and I learned the importance of letting go and attending to the reality that is happening now rather than sticking to an agenda. We faced our own fear of failing and leapt into the unknown. We found that we were actually grateful for the mess that had arisen, since it built new muscle in the organization for facing differences along the uncertain path ahead."

Rather than seeing strategy as a way to control a process or to expect a particular outcome, we can step back and attend to the current reality of what is. Rather than follow slavishly what we have planned, we can work with what we already have. One of the keys to this is giving voice to what is unsaid, so that people can be heard. What can seem to be a silent blockage to change can suddenly become known and worked with, through dialogue.

A word of caution, though. **We need to be careful about what we let go of.** Tied up in that are complexities concerning our agency and competency. Sometimes the temptation is to throw out too much of what we know. When a colleague of Diana's started in a role that was new to her, requiring her to develop new skills and expertise, she felt that everything she had acquired that had got her to that point was no longer useful in her new context. She had assumed that all the things she had learnt in the previous position, such as management and strategy, had no place in her new role. Only later did she realize that she had thrown out too much and had stopped trusting what she knew. This had an impact on her confidence and ability to contribute the breadth of her experience.

5.

SAY "I DON'T KNOW"

"To admit to ignorance, uncertainty or ambivalence is to cede your place on the masthead, your slot on the programme, and allow all the coveted eyeballs to turn instead to the next hack who's more than happy to sell them all the answers."

American essayist and cartoonist Tim Kreider

Why is Not Knowing so hard? To move forward in situations of uncertainty we have to cross the threshold, the edge at "Finisterre." And the only way to do that is to make a simple but devilishly hard statement: "I don't know."

Legend goes that Socrates' friend Chaerephon asked the Delphic Oracle whether anyone was wiser than Socrates. When the answer came back that there was none wiser in the whole of Athens, Socrates set out on a mission to solve the paradox. How could he, a man so profoundly ignorant, be considered to be the wisest man of all? He spoke to politicians, poets and other elites, and realized that they were all pretending to have knowledge and wisdom. Socrates concluded that the Oracle was right. Unlike everyone else, he knew that he was ignorant, which made him wise: *"I know one thing: that I know nothing."*

Can we accept that we don't know? Can we admit that we don't know? Can we deliberately acknowledge and enter into a space where our frame of reference is "I don't know"? So when the boss says – "I looked at the data and I know that if we take this course of action sales will rise" – we can say – "This is a new market, so we can't be sure. Let's try a variety of things." Or when we attend a meeting that goes over our heads, rather than go along with it all and pretend that we understand the issues and agree to the actions, can we say "I am not yet decided. Can we discuss this further?" This may be unsettling, especially if we are leading others who have a key decision making role. As Nicolas Petrovic, CEO of Eurostar, says: *the managers who can't tolerate ambiguity are those that feel lost when you answer 'it depends'.*

It is hard not to know when people are looking to us to supply the answers. Tim Kreider describes the dilemma facing journalists like him: *"The one thing no editorialist or commentator in any media is ever supposed to say is 'I don't know': that they're too ignorant about the science of climate change to have an informed opinion; that they frankly have no idea what to do about gun violence in this country; or that they've just never quite understood the Israeli-Palestinian conflict and in all honesty they're sick of hearing about it."*[70]

Quoting British psychoanalyst Wilfred Bion, academics Robert French and Peter Simpson argue that if we can resist the temptation to fill in with knowing the space that is created by ignorance, we allow for new ideas, thoughts and insights to emerge.[71]

This doesn't mean that we need to forget everything, or deny what we already know. It rather means that we can hold our knowledge and our ideas lightly. Bion provides the metaphor that we need a "binocular vision" – keeping both what we know and what we don't know in focus at the same time.

When Francisca Perez, an experienced scientist from Spain, recently moved from a science-led pharmaceutical company to a commercial tourism firm in Switzerland, she found resistance to her usual Not Knowing approach. *"From my scientist perspective, 'I don't know' was synonymous with 'I'm confident' (only insecure people need to fake it) and 'you can trust me' (because I will tell you exactly what I know and what I don't)."*

However, she quickly came to realize that those words had a completely different meaning in the business world. She was now working in a fast-paced industry, in a role where her input could have a very direct impact on business results. It was fundamental that she knew and could supply certainties. *"In this new context, saying 'I don't know' was the equivalent of saying 'I'm not suitable for the job'."* For the first time in her life, Francisca found herself in a situation where she did not have the permission to not know. For a number of months she silently wondered every day whether she would make the mistake that would result in her eventually being fired. Francisca has since adapted to the new environment and learned how to balance the tension between her internal openness to Not Knowing and the outside pressure to know.

In spite of the potential risks, admitting that we don't know can develop a sense of connection with those around us. The vulnerability and humility in that admission can bring us closer to the people we work with, and can engage them in the challenge of moving forward and trying to solve the problem at hand. The power differential and the hierarchical structure become inconsequential when we are facing our biggest challenges together.

Glenn Fernandez, a former senior sales manager at an international dairy company, found himself leading a new team after a restructure. He recalls: *"I didn't know how to engage these people that had lost half of their work due to the change in business strategy. They used to be a high-performing team, but now they seemed disengaged, lacking drive and purpose. Managing people through a period of uncertainty is a tough gig, and the key executive that had faith in me had left the organization, so I had no support. This is where I went 'holy shit'! This is where I felt the most vulnerable. I had lost my way, and my biggest supporter and advocate was not there... I shrunk in my shell. I struggled for several weeks, turning up to work and doing stuff, not understanding my purpose. I felt insecure. I really had no idea what to do with this new team. I was in this dark spot and I swirled around it for a while, with no guidance from anyone."*

One day Glenn decided to take the team away and create a space to talk about what was going on. They went on a two-day off-site trip. He decided to take the risk of sharing that he felt insecure, how he'd been waiting for someone to tell him what to do. He confided in them that he did not know how to deal with the situation, that he had more questions than answers. It was the first time that he had opened up to a new team about his vulnerabilities and he was really nervous. The organization had a top-down, micromanagement culture. None of his managers had ever shared their insecurities with him.

"The message to them was – 'I trust you, I respect you,' and they got it. What happened was that sharing with them how I felt opened up the space for them to also share their story with the group. Everyone had the same reaction to the changes, insecurity, self-doubt... it was a shared experience that galvanized the team. Saying **'I don't know' is a great leveller.***"*

The act of saying "I don't know" sends a clear signal to others that this is a situation where existing knowledge will not be our guide. It gives us and others permission to look for other ways, to be a beginner again. Acknowledging our limitations is incredibly liberating. As Jean-Jacques Rousseau writes, *"I do not know is a phrase which becomes us."*

6.

ENTERTAIN DOUBT

"To believe fully and at the same moment to have doubts is not at all a contradiction: it presupposes a greater respect for truth, an awareness that truth always goes beyond anything that can be said or done at any given moment."

American existential psychologist Rollo May

Diana: *In coaching sessions I often hear my clients grapple with the question "How do I know I'm right?" It is the hardest question to hear and one of the most challenging to work with. Many of these people have high-powered jobs and heavy decision-making responsibilities....We carve out our lives in right and wrongs, black and white. We look for a sign, any sign, that shows us we are heading in the "right" direction. Can we entertain the possibility of doubt?*

Business thinker and author Charles Handy, now 81, describes himself as a social philosopher. In a conversation Steven had with Charles and his wife, Liz, Charles recalled a meeting at the London Business School when they were choosing who to promote from a lecturer to a professor. There was one candidate who people knew was not right, but they could not put their finger on exactly why this was so. Then someone said: *"The problem with him is that he has no decent doubt."*

"It's OK to have decent doubt," said Charles. *"Those who advocate certainty are not credible. This is the nature of faith, having some belief that all will be well, even in the uncertainty."* He recalled Julian of Norwich, the medieval English mystic, who summed up *"All shall be well, and all manner of things shall be well."* This much-loved saying holds much hope for us – that even if we don't understand and are confused in the midst of uncertainty, we will be OK in the end.

Reliance on our existing knowledge can often trap us – especially when new information comes along. The best academics and leaders entertain doubt about their own state of knowledge. This helps them open up new discoveries and creates "pockets" of Not Knowing.

The ability to question as a matter of habit, to admit that the lens through which we are looking at the world is subjective and flawed, is an essential leadership skill. Doubting the outcome of a project can free us up to engage with others and invite in different views that add new insights into complex challenges. It can help us make better decisions.

Carsten Sudhoff, the former Chief HR Officer of the World Economic Forum and founder of Circular Society, recalls a night in Dubai where everything changed for him. He'd arrived in the iconic UAE city the night before the annual summit on the Global Agenda of the World Economic Forum.

"It must have been the overall ambiance and the heat, as well as the intensity of our conversation that triggered a deep state of questioning. Was leadership, or the absence of it, really the only cause for the many large-scale issues society faces? Or was leadership a derivative of a larger societal imbalance? In a world dominated by complexity and ambiguity, where the environment, societies and economies are so obviously interconnected, can we really continue this exclusive focus on individual success?"

Carsten hypothesized that many of the burning issues could be resolved if people considered their interconnectedness with others. He had no idea if his hypothesis was correct, but the thought of bringing the "reality of interconnectedness" into the realm of leadership and societal development was intriguing.

"That night, I could not sleep. I had so many questions circulating in my mind: If this hypothesis is true, how can societal change be brought about? How should I proceed? Am I just too naïve?"

When he returned to Switzerland, Carsten began drafting a vision in a white paper. An experienced senior executive, he was adept at formulating strategic documents, but it quickly became clear that this one was going to be very different. This time he was writing about his personal dream, his vision for a better world, where individuals and institutions could achieve success and satisfaction as they improved the lives of others. *"With every line I wrote I saw the vastness of the unknown expanding in front of me. Every finished chapter produced more questions that I did not know the answers for. Doubt settled in. It felt both a frightening yet extremely energizing space to be in."*

Carsten realized that this was not just another project; it was his dream, his calling, and it might mean giving up his role at the World Economic Forum to make it become a reality. He was plagued by doubt. *"Do I have what it takes to be an entrepreneur? I had a track record of creativity and persistence. But was that enough? I had succeeded in different organizational settings. But could I survive without corporate support and on my own? Could I earn a living this way?"*

As he opened up and shared his doubts with some of his entrepreneur friends, he understood that the anxiety he was experiencing and his self-doubts were absolutely normal and healthy for anyone in that situation. *"They did not necessarily have the answers to my questions but the discussion helped me frame and shape the issues. There was no such thing as a perfect script for me to follow."* Carsten has since left the World Economic Forum and started Circular Society, a social enterprise that aims to drive a new way of thinking and acting to improve life perspectives for individuals and society as a whole.

Doubt is a doorway to possibility and admitting doubt shows flexibility and openness to learning and creativity. However, let's not confuse that with a lack of belief in ourselves. The assumption that admitting doubt is a weakness is a barrier to engaging with Not Knowing. We don't want people to see the more unsure part of ourselves – we assume that if people saw our doubt, they would lose faith in us and we don't like the way this thought makes us feel. In a recent biography of George W Bush[72] it was revealed that in spite of his public steadfast certainty about the Iraq war, even he privately showed doubt. What stopped Bush from admitting his doubt publicly was his view that leaders must show certainty in order to be credible and to be taken seriously.

7.

WORK WITH RESISTANCE

When he received his first book publishing contract, author and entrepreneur Nick Williams, whose story appeared earlier (see page 124), struggled with a strong inner voice of resistance. This voice was telling him that he was not up to the job of writing, that he would not be successful at the task. Yet at the same time he recognized another, weaker, voice that said: *"You were born to write, you can do this."*

Nick left the envelope with the contract offer open and took time to "be" with his resistance. But instead of listening to this voice of resistance, he became curious and started to question it. He went into silence and touched deeply into what it was that he was afraid of. He took the time to listen to his heart and reconnect with the dreams and desires of the eight-year-old child who'd asked for writing pens for Christmas: *"I don't know that souls can scream, but I felt as if my soul was screaming at me, 'Write the bloody book! It's part of your calling, and what you are here for!'"* Nick recalls.

After a few days he said a prayer and signed the contract. The resistance was still there, but during that period of reflection, Nick connected with his calling. He learned how to be with his resistance without allowing it to take him over.

In that moment of commitment of signing the contract, a door to inspiration opened for him. Nick started writing between three and 13 hours a day for the next three months. He handed in two carrier bags of manuscript, on time, in January 1999.

The book came out in September 1999 and become a best-seller.

BEING IN THE DARK IS

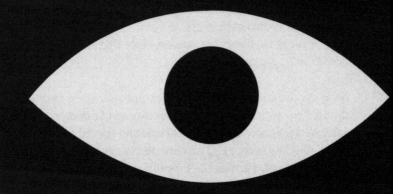

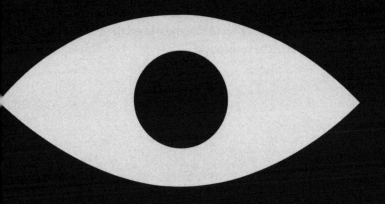

A SPACE FULL OF POTENTIAL

Nick reflects: *"I have learned that the unknown need not be so scary because it is always pregnant with opportunity and possibility. Venture your heart – take the risk to discover who you truly are and the difference you can make."*

Nick also learned that sometimes we need to give up all hope of being ready and confident enough to take on the really big things in our lives. Success for him came from starting before he felt ready and unfurling his wings as he went along. As he became aware of his greatest fears and moved in that direction to confront them, he discovered that most good things exist just on the other side of the resistance.

8.

EMBODIED NOT KNOWING

Being brought up by teachers and with a precocious reading habit, Mark Walsh, 'Embodied Leadership' trainer, found school and academic learning straightforward. He grew up thinking that this was the only way to learn that mattered – at least until he took his driving test, an important milestone of practical importance in rural East Anglia, UK. He failed the test dismally, several times. He recalls one occasion when he was driven back to the test centre by the examiner on his insistence for their safety. Around the same time, Mark also fell madly in first love and discovered the world of connection and intensity of feeling within the body. *"The world of love knocked me off the scholastic pedestal and brought me to my senses."* Sadly, inexperienced in relationships, he soon "failed" in this area too. It turned out that there was a lot he didn't know.

"What these two hard lessons showed me is that there are other ways to be smart than cognitively 'knowing about'," Mark says. *"Driving and social relations are not things you can learn from a book. They are examples of what neuroscientists now call implicit, procedural or embodied learning. Leadership, relationships and life itself are an embodied matter. The body is our unconscious and it reveals itself through habit and intuition. If we limit ourselves to what we know about, we limit access to what we really know."*

Mark discovered this through bodily arts such as martial arts and dance that he has since studied. However, in the modern work environment where he trains and consults, he has found that people often ignore the body. True effectiveness through responsiveness and creativity only comes through relaxing and letting the intuitive bodily response flow. In Zen this is known as "Mushin" or "no-mind." This concept is familiar to actors, comedy improvisers, lovers and great leaders. Mark explains: *"The body is a source of both mystery and wisdom. This may be surprising to those accustomed to viewing the body simply as a cart that carries the brain around. So I should first explain that when I say 'body', I do not just think of a machine but rather an intimate part of who we are. How we move and how we stand is the way we are in the world."*

Mark notes that the illusion of knowing both the world and ourselves is maintained in our literal leanings and movement patterns. We have habits and the body keeps these in place. *"From the perspective of Not Knowing, our bodily predispositions – solidifications of past events – take us away from the reality of what actually is and from flexibility of response. If we are not in dialogue with what may be, but rather repeating patterns from the past, we cannot respond with power and grace."*

The body is a gateway to Not Knowing, a useful resource to tap into when our heads and brains fail us in the confusion and anxiety of the unknown. Rather than try to "work things out" in our usual, habitual ways, only to find out that we can't, we can practise being more embodied. What happens "below the neck" is crucial as a source of data for what is going on, as well as for giving us clues in navigating the unknown.

9.

PREPARE THE GROUND

In 2000 the US Newspaper industry revenue was $65 billion. By 2012 this had dropped to approximately $20 billion. A morbid website sprang up – newspaperdeathwatch.com. In the UK, 242 local newspapers disappeared in the seven years from 2005. This was not a change that CEOs were used to; it was something completely different. No one knew what was next or what they were going to do.

One newspaper that has managed to weather the storm is the *Financial Times*, published in the UK for an international readership. With its distinctive pink paper, the *FT*, as it is affectionately known amongst its loyal readers, provides market-sensitive information and high-quality journalism to the business world.

Steven and a colleague have been working with Ben Hughes, deputy global CEO of the *FT* and Global Commercial Director, and his management team for the past three years. Ben describes how the *FT* learned to manage the transition from the known (print) world to the new unknown (digital) world.

"Although I had seen this gradual trend, it really hit home to me in the summer of 2012 when our online revenues and circulation passed our print revenues and circulation for the first time. I remember looking at a 35-slide strategy presentation and only one slide was devoted to print circulation and advertising. In a very short space of time our print circulation in the US dropped rapidly. This was the moment of the 'tilt' and business would not be the same after that."

The *FT* signalled its intentions internally with the slogan "Digital First." The senior leadership team met quarterly over several years to engage in what the business could do to prepare for the complexity surrounding changes in the industry. The changes were happening so fast that even radical ideas were put forward. The finance director was adamant that *FT* could succeed as a business without print and maintain a viable online business.

The team had to manage the tension between embracing the future and recognizing and honouring the past. They decided that it was not a case of choosing the future over the past, but of being able to re-purpose the present print business and explore new opportunities in the digital arena simultaneously. Although print revenue has shrunk, it still contributes an important and significant income to the business.

"While I believe that we must do all we can to clearly and decisively embrace the future, I think one of the mistakes of leaders working with the unknown is to dismiss and not to honour the present enough," says Ben.

To strengthen the business, the *FT* reaffirmed what it was originally known for – high-quality editorial content. *FT* columnists are known for their integrity and depth of analysis and moreover the unreliability of information published on the internet has triggered a flight to quality by readers willing to pay for it. This was highlighted during the 2012/2013 Leveson Inquiry into the UK press that resulted from the phone-hacking scandal in 2011 and the revelation of highly dubious journalistic practices. The *FT* remained unblemished.

Like all newspapers, the *FT* has had to make changes to staff numbers. Ben recalls a moment of truth for staff at the paper: *"One of the most important lessons in working with the unknown for us was about being open and honest in communication. I remember speaking to a group of staff after they had seen a change in numbers of staff. I told them that I really wished I could sit in front of them and promise that this is the end of change but I could not tell them this. I told them that while other companies might not appear to be making changes, we didn't think ignoring the future was an option."*

Ben and the *FT* senior leadership team were able to prepare the staff for the changes ahead, and make the transition to a new reality by building a bridge between the past and the future. They created a safe enough space for people to manage their anxiety about the unknowns ahead by honouring what they were good at, building on the existing strong structures of the business, and communicating openly and honestly. By honouring the loss of what was the case in the past and celebrating the potential opportunities that lay ahead of them, the *FT* was able to ride the wave of change in the industry rather than be swamped by it.

Another way to prepare the ground for the unknown is to demonstrate "skin in the game." This signals an unwavering commitment to the journey ahead that inspires and motivates others to follow. Sherry Coutu is one of the world's experts in bridging technology, entrepreneurship and education. She has been recognized by Wired magazine in the top 25 most influential people in the technology world. She holds board and advisory positions including Raspberry Pi, Founders4schools, LinkedIn, Artfinder, Care.com, and Cambridge University Press.

Sherry has a strong track record of bringing together stakeholders to make things happen. Recently she founded "The Cambridge Cluster Map," a company that takes data from Companies House and LinkedIn to produce a map of which companies are growing the fastest. To date over 1,540 companies, totalling £12.3 billion, have been mapped.

"This was a difficult project as it involved getting data from government, which has additional layers of complication," says Sherry. *"One of the key things that helped this project succeed was demonstrating a firm commitment in the face of the unknown.*

Putting in my own money to back the project. Others came in when they could see how I was committed personally."

Some sponsors were happy to come on board if Sherry got three companies to commit to the project. However, her accomplishment was that she managed to get all six that she wanted. She explains that one key lesson she learned from this experience was that we do not know what we are capable of until we hear other people's stories. *"Often the simple fact of exposure can be the seed that leads to discovery of more and the fulfilment of potential that otherwise may have gone untapped."*

Sherry's ability to demonstrate "skin in the game" gave confidence to others to come on board and invest in a high-risk venture that had many unknowns.

CLOSE YOUR EYES
TO SEE

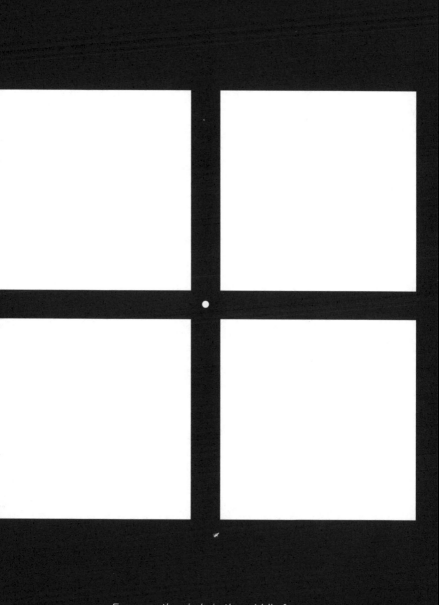

CHAPTER 7

*Focus on the circle in the middle for
about 30 seconds, then close your eyes.
What do you see?*

"I shut my eyes   in order to see."

Paul Gauguin

1.

CLOSE YOUR EYES TO SEE

Marco Antonio Martinez is a Mexican photographer who has exhibited in galleries around the world. One project visualizes a dream he had, which he created by moulding small sculptures with clay and aluminium and building scenes. One photograph shows a red tunnel scattered with small beetle-like creatures, drifting into an abyss. They cast eerie shadows, creating a surreal and beautiful dreamscape. Another photo in the series has softly glowing trees across a dark background with their delicate light trails. In another, a proud shining Pegasus appears in a spot of light in the darkness.

In a video presentation of the photo project, Marco Antonio describes the Pegasus as a strong and free creature. He remembers that in the dream the Pegasus transmits these feelings to him, a liberation after the claustrophobia of the abyss in the first photo in the essay. The dream suddenly ends in a flash of red light.

These photos are beautiful and haunting; they are also extraordinary because Marco Antonio is blind. And the dream he describes through his photos occurred only seven days after he suddenly became blind. This story can give us an insight into the internal experience of blindness in a way that no rational description can.

Before his blindness Marco Antonio almost never used a camera and like most people, he only took casual pictures, such as family photos at parties. He hadn't been interested in art photography at all.

"When you become blind you feel somehow lost," he says. *"Life forces you to solve new problems or concerns that you never even dreamt of before. This is very frustrating. Inevitably you have to learn alternatives, tools and new skills. It forces you to explore at all times, to make you more aware of your space and yourself. You acknowledge that learning by trial and error is part of the process."*

Through the techniques of sensory photography, together with his previous visual references, Marco Antonio learned how to create images. *"Imagining my environment is essential for me to feel and understand where I am. Now I imagine constantly, which enables me to expand my reality, one where I build and design all the time."*

Marco Antonio learned photography at *"Ojos Que Sienten"* or *"Sight of Emotion,"* a social organization in Mexico City. It is an ambitious project to teach photography to blind people and change the mainstream's perception towards people with visual impairments. The organization has worked with over 1,000 young people in Mexico and also runs projects globally.

The photography process pioneered at "Sight of Emotion" involves visually impaired people using all their senses to create a road map in order to produce an image. Sound is a reference for the photographers to know where the subject matter is and also to identify distances and heights. To frame the photo, they open their arms at an angle of 75° to 80° because that is the angle of view of point-and-shoot digital cameras. Using touch, they can gather additional information, such as the texture of the object, and the length and type of hair of their subjects, for example. For street photography, smell is also an important reference point for what is going on around the photographer.

The project was started by Mexican photographer Gina Badenoch: *"When walking into the unknown, the worst thing you can do is to hold on to your ego wanting to control what you cannot control,"* Gina comments. Through her work she asks partici-pants to accept their present situation, identify and accept what they do not have, but instead focus on what they still do have, and acknowledge ways in which working with others can com-plement their present weaknesses.

For most photographers the output, the photographic print, is the whole point of photography. But for visually impaired peo-ple, the point is the process itself and the printed photo is for others to appreciate. The photographers immerse themselves and appreciate the whole process of taking a photo, as well as the intense satisfaction they can receive from someone else loving it.

Gina reflects: *"Throughout the years I have witnessed a lot of stories that have been told around the world through photographs taken with all the other senses by blind people. I have also seen lives transformed because people who had become invisible were now not only being included, but enhancing our visual world."*

In a business context, relying on a certain kind of market in-formation from a certain source may limit the weight we give to other sources of information, and blind us from the value of other, seemingly less important, sources or senses.

Steven: I was once in Innsbruck, Austria, with a friend and went to Discover your Senses, a city experience in complete darkness. After paying for our tickets, we were led to a waiting area where we were blindfolded and introduced to our guides. With a hand hold-ing me under the elbow, I was guided as I stepped forward through doors. No light could be sensed through the blindfold – nothing to provide a sense of orientation. I felt scared and exhilarated at the same time.

As I walked my hand reached out in front of me involuntari-ly, feeling my way, trying to avoid hitting something and hurt-ing myself. Progress was slow as I took tentative steps forward, cautiously trying to sense where I was. As I became more comfortable with not seeing, my other senses kicked in. I became aware of the soft ground beneath me, cushioning my steps. I smelled freshly cut grass, then a subtle smell of flowers drifted past me, with the breeze. Was I in a field? I could hear the soft murmurs of a river and the sound grew stronger as I edged nearer. I listened intently, and felt a heightened awareness of my movements.

My guide's hand would gently beckon me forward if I stopped or hesitated. The guides' banter in the background created a reassuring feeling. Over the course of the next hour we went over a bridge, crossed a busy street where I could hear the terrifying sounds of the traffic, walked past a busy marketplace and a church ringing its bells, then arrived at what seemed to be our final destination – a restaurant where we would order, eat and even pay in the dark. Without sight to guide my meal, I slowed down and savoured every mouthful. The sense of smell became alive and my tongue felt the nuance in textures as if for the first time, while my hands would frequently touch the plate, to make sure it was still there!

At the end of the meal we were led through a door into the exit where we were finally able to remove our blindfolds. As my eyes grew accustomed to the light again, I was shocked to realize that the guides that had taken us around so expertly were blind. Although this experience was over a decade ago, it remains fresh and vivid to this day.

Following the selective blindness approach, we might deliberately turn off some sources of information to learn more from surprising sources, where our direct experience comes into play. For example, we might look at our new employees as a source of information, rather than go to the usual trusted sources.

Closing the eyes in order to see is a way of shutting off some knowledge, deliberately Not Knowing from an important source, to open up a new knowing in a place we haven't been before. Paradoxically, this shutting down creates new knowledge. That is one secret to Not Knowing – far from reducing knowledge, the process is generative, creating knowledge in new ways that unlocks tough challenges that the old knowledge couldn't address.

2.
OBSERVE

"The real voyage of discovery consists not in seeking new landscapes, but in having new eyes."

Author Marcel Proust

Most of us have had that wonderful experience of travelling to new lands and feeling the excitement of "what's around the corner?" Enjoying a new place, a new cuisine or new smells. It's the perspective of the foreigner. Yet how can we take the same approach when confronting the unknown in our daily lives? Alain de Botton calls this a "travelling mindset,"[73] a quality embodied by Xavier de Maistre, a Frenchman who in 1795 pioneered a new mode of travel: room-travel.

De Maistre's thirst for adventure took him from his place of birth at the foot of the French Alps to Turin in Italy, then to St Petersburg in Russia, where he spent the last years of his life. He is also known to have attempted air travel in his 20s, when he built large wings out of paper, ambitiously planning to cross the Atlantic to America. His daring adventure did not come about, but instead, in 1790 De Maistre embarked on an adventure of a different kind, when he found himself under house arrest for 42 days as a punishment for participating in a duel. He set out to discover his bedroom, chronicling the journey in the book *Voyage autour de ma chambre*, or *Journey around my bedroom*.

In the book he describes how he meanders through the room, slowly and non-linearly taking in the "sights," writing in the style of the travel books of the era: *"Once you've left my armchair, walking towards the north, you come into view of my bed."* He explains his approach to his journey: *"I will trace out every possible geometrical trajectory if need be. . . . My soul is so open to every kind of idea, taste, and sentiment; it so avidly receives everything that presents itself!"*

De Maistre's ability to observe neutrally, to re-discover the known and the familiar, and his painstaking attention to detail are wonderful examples of a mindset that would serve us well more than 200 years later.

The process of observation slows us down and grounds us in the present moment. It can help us resist the temptation to jump to action, into solution mode, too quickly. When we keenly observe what is around us, what is going on, we can gain a better perspective in the midst of action. Marco Antonio Martinez likes describing the act of observation as a *"stimulation of all our senses."* He believes that this definition enables us to have a better view of challenging things and situations. *"In life there are unknown situations which can paralyze us and push us to believe that it is impossible to do something about them. If we learn to observe things with our other senses, finding different and new perspectives, we can find new ways to achieve our dreams."*

When we are trying to make sense of a situation, or make progress with a complex challenge, rather than relying just with our intellect, we can engage all our senses in a process of observation. We can immerse ourselves in the experience and collect information through any sense that is available to us – sight, hearing, smell, touch or taste. This rich data can provide us with more options for engaging with the issue at hand. The more detached we can become in our observations, without being influenced by our thoughts, feelings, prejudices or interpretations, the more we can be open to a new space of inquiry and wonder.

There are many spiritual practices that have developed awareness teachings such as mindfulness in Buddhism and contemplation in action in the Catholic tradition. They all serve to help us step back and ask "where am I?" or "what's going on here?" Simple acts such as pushing our chair back in a meeting, focusing on our breath for a few moments, or developing a practice of debriefing can bring us a little closer to becoming more observant and reflective.

3.

CREATE SPACE FOR SILENCE

*"To arrive at the simplest truth,
as Newton knew and practised, requires
years of contemplation. Not activity.
Not reasoning. Not calculating.
Not busy behaviour of any kind. Not
reading. Not talking. Not making any
effort. Not thinking. Simply bearing in
mind what it is one needs to know."*

Mathematician G Spencer Brown

Silence may be tough in a corporate setting, but what could be a more hostile environment than a Latin-American prison? For the past two and a half years, José Keith Romero has introduced meditation practices into Mexican prisons. The purpose of his volunteer work has been to build up and strengthen the experience of internal peace, self-esteem and respect within the interned population.

Recently José and his team were in a large penitentiary in Mexico City, in the space assigned to prisoners for meditation. There were no windows, no ventilation and the place felt oppressive. They'd brought in a laptop in order to play meditative music and break through the noise of the facility. On this particular day, as they started the meditation programme, in the midst of chanting, the computer stopped working. The inmates waited patiently for the team of volunteers to fix it. However, after a few desperate attempts they gave up and started chanting acappella instead.

SILENCE

To José's utter surprise, the inmates responded in harmony. *"It was as if they were actively requesting guidance from the power of the chant. The melody of voices danced through all corners of the room."* After 15 minutes of chanting, they entered into silence and meditation. It was a simple practice of deep breathing, posture and the silence of the mind. *"We entered into this sacred space of nothingness. Deep breathing took over, no sound, no chant, just the sound of the breath, coming in and out, in total harmony."*

At the end, one of the facilitators invited everyone to open their eyes, wiggle their toes, make contact with their body, and bring their consciousness back into the room. The programme came to an end, everyone shook hands goodbye and the volunteer team moved out through the winding corridors.

"As we walked out of the prison gates," José recalls, *"we contemplated what had just happened. At the core, the universe does not need laptops, tape recorders, or sound to make itself known. When you quiet the mind, surrender the soul to the wisdom of the heart, the future comes in; and peace and respect simply merge."*

There is something powerful in collective silence that connects and transports us. When the unexpected occurs, throwing us off course, or when things are not working for us, rather than scramble to "fill in the void," to do something, we can slow down and become silent, just pausing and waiting. The few seconds may feel like an eternity but the silence can open up a space for something new to emerge. In time this can become a practice that enables us to accept what is and that reduces our instinct to take control.

Silence as discernment

The Society of Friends, better known as The Quakers, has a great tradition of using silence to centre before working together. Author, educator and activist Parker Palmer tells of one such event: *"At one community meeting, we ran into a high-conflict issue. We ran out of time and agreed to postpone this issue until the following week. All week emotions ran high and opposing views intensified. We eagerly assembled at the next meeting, impatient to get this issue resolved. This was a Quaker community – each meeting began with five minutes of silence. On this day, the clerk announced that, due to the intensity of this issue, we would not begin with our usual five minutes of silence. We all breathed a sigh of relief, only to hear her announce: "Today, we'll begin with 20 minutes of silence."*[74]

Bruce "Harv" Busta, a senior professor of accounting at St Cloud State University in Minnesota and a professional auditor, illustrates how silence can be used to find time to listen to oneself when facing a difficult situation.

"I am a Quaker. We believe that God can and does speak directly to us. We sit in silent contemplation and listen . . . to God, to ourselves, to each other. We listen in silence to discern the right path. Listening requires practice. We start by letting go of our knowledge, agenda and concerns to 'centre down' and focus on listening. We are listening for openings of our heart and mind."

For Harv the discernment process is slow. It is not typically a flash of insight and a quick answer to a problem. Rather, it is repetitive process where the mind becomes quiet and one waits in careful expectation for clarity; as Harv puts it, less fuzziness.

One day Harv sat in his office and stared at the piles of research opportunities he had collected. As a fully tenured professor he had reached a point in his career where he had one major research effort remaining. The question was: which one? There were many interesting and worthwhile avenues to pursue, many that deeply interested him, but given the numbers of years he had left, he knew he only had time to follow one of these paths seriously. This was a perfect opportunity for Harv to use silence for discernment.

"So looking for clearness... I begin. Sitting in silence, thinking about my decision, then trying not to think about my decision... just trying to let the silence flow over me, wash me. Breathing slowly, listening. Relaxing, clearing my mind. My decision creeps back into my thinking, I gently push it away and re-centre, not thinking about it, not thinking about anything, just listening. By clearing the mind, slowly, very slowly the mind runs out of thoughts. You become open to hearing the stirrings of a message. Clarity can occur here. It is like a muddy pool, by doing nothing, by leaving it alone, the mud will settle. The same is true of our thoughts, by thinking of nothing, the confusion settles and clarity can come. Twenty minutes, 30 minutes... What happens? Lightning bolt? Clear message from God?... well, usually very little; however, the silence and letting go leaves you more comforted and calm."

Over time, perhaps several months, slowly, Harv started getting small bits of clarity, pieces of the puzzle about which research path was best for him and those around him. *"This path is the one that God wants me to follow, not necessarily the one that I expected or hoped for."* Harv explains that it is important that the process of discernment also involves people we trust and can confide in, with whom we can explore our decision. The role of others is not to give advice or guidance but rather to help us look at the issue from several viewpoints, discussing obstacles and impediments.

"Discernment is more than insight or good judgement. It is not an intellectual exercise of determining an outcome. It is a process of seeking and listening to hear an inner sacred voice. It is clearing our minds and opening ourselves to hearing the stirrings of a message."

4.

LISTEN

Research shows that doctors typically wait only **23 seconds** after a patient begins describing their chief complaint before interrupting and redirecting the discussion. A study carried out by Dr Howard Beckman and his colleagues from the University of Rochester Medical Center showed that the low quality of the doctors' listening before redirecting the conversation can lead to missed opportunities to gather important data.[75] The study also found that the patients would have been able to talk about all of their concerns if the doctors had waited only **six more seconds** before starting to ask questions. As doctors usually interrupted after the first concern was expressed, many patients failed to bring up other important issues.

Otto Scharmer, Senior Lecturer at MIT and founding chair of the Presencing Institute, is the originator of "Theory U," a process based on a concept he calls "Presencing." Presencing is described as a heightened state of attention that allows individuals and groups to shift the inner place from which they function so they can begin operating from the emerging space of possibility.[76] In Theory U Scharmer describes four types of listening:[77]

Downloading, where we are purely listening to reconfirm our judgements. "I know that already." We are looking for what we already know.

Factual, where we are paying attention to the facts to gather more data. We are looking for what we don't already know.

Empathic, where we are able to listen with an open heart and connect with another person by engaging in real dialogue and paying careful attention to them and their story. We forget about our own agenda and see the world through their eyes.

Generative, where we connect at a deeper level, and to something larger than ourselves. This experience is hard to describe; it has an "out of this world" quality, where things slow down and we are fully present to what is unfolding.

Nadine McCarthy is a corporate coach in Ireland. In 2006, while still a trainee coach, she worked on a project involving a CEO client of a leading Irish organization. The CEO's 360-degree performance feedback showed strong leadership but lower levels of competency in being at ease and stress-free in the job. In a coaching session with Nadine the CEO identified the main cause of this lower level of competency as high and unrealistic expectations of herself and others, and the stress of putting in extremely long working hours. Given the CEO's strong leadership qualities, Nadine was shocked to hear her express this as *"nothing I do is good enough, nor will it ever be."* Nadine remembers feeling increasingly frustrated with herself during the coaching session, and getting mentally distracted at her own inability to help her client. The more she probed and asked questions, the more anxious the CEO seemed to get.

"Suddenly, I became aware in that moment that I was in fact listening to myself rather than my client. I was listening to the voice in my own head, worrying about how I could help her, questioning whether I was a good coach, wondering what she thought of me now, that it was obvious I was only a trainee coach."

In the midst of this turmoil Nadine remembered that the CEO had mentioned her father a number of times during the session. Nadine decided to follow this lead, but this time she decided to listen not just to the words, but to be fully present to how her client was sitting, breathing and her facial expressions.

"I stayed like this, just listening to her until I felt every part of me was listening to her, trusting that the right next step would

unfold. As I listened in this way, it was as if every word she was saying lit up and I could see it in my mind's eye. I then heard her saying that she just needed to learn to relax."

Nadine took this cue and guided her client through a visualization to allow her body and mind to relax. Gradually the CEO's features softened and her breathing slowed down. Afterwards tears appeared in her eyes and she started recalling a powerful memory of her father. She described a time when she had just received the results of her first university degree: *"I had achieved a 2:1 (high second-class honours) in my degree and I was thrilled. I had gone home to celebrate with my parents. As my dad opened a celebratory bottle of champagne, he said: 'It's a pity you didn't get a first!'"* As she said those words, the CEO stopped, sat in stunned silence and then looked at Nadine, blinking and shaking her head with a newfound insight into why she had been driving herself relentlessly for the past 26 years. Nadine reflects: *"Something really magical happened in the coaching session when I surrendered to Not Knowing and truly listened."*

Generative listening is as old as the world's ancient cultures. We can learn from the Aboriginal people of Australia, the world's oldest indigenous culture, who learn by sitting, listening, watching and waiting. This is called *"dadirri."* Miriam-Rose Ungunmerr-Baumann, artist and tribal Aboriginal elder from the Daly River in the Northern Territory, describes this special quality as *"inner, deep listening and quiet, still awareness."*[78]

"Dadirri recognizes the deep spring that is inside us... A big part of dadirri is listening ...When I experience dadirri, I am made whole again. I can sit on the riverbank or walk through the trees; even if someone close to me has passed away, I can find my peace in this silent awareness. There is no need of words. My people are not threatened by silence. They are completely at home in it. They have lived for thousands of years with Nature's quietness."[79]

5.

CHALLENGE ASSUMPTIONS

*"The enemy of art is assumption.
The assumption that you know what you
are doing, the assumption that you know
how to walk and how to talk,
the assumption that what you 'mean'
will mean the same thing to those who
receive it."*

Theatre director Anne Bogart

When Mobin Asghar Rana, a 31-year-old from Pakistan, took up a management field sales role for a major FMCG in Saudi Arabia, he knew he was venturing into new territory. *"I need to do things differently and take risks to make it interesting in my personal and professional life. I believe my faith also gives me strength in questioning the 'unknown space'. I like the biblical parable of the birds who do not worry where their next meal will come. It indicates a natural basic trust despite our worry."*

Although he was comfortable entering the unknown, having grown up in a competitive environment that encouraged an exploratory mindset in his career and life, Mobin knew this would be a completely new challenge. He was in a new country, he did not speak the language and found himself in charge of a new team of people.

"I was nervous, but I think my new colleagues were even more nervous. Many of us are comfortable working with people of similar

Hell

GO LEFT

GO RIGHT

Heaven

style and culture and have preconceived notions that others who are not from our cultural group may not be able to understand us."

Mobin found the stereotypes that his team held about his culture challenging to work with, in particular the belief held by some that the Arab culture is superior to the South Asian culture. *"These beliefs come from experiences accumulated over many years as a large amount of working class manual labour has been coming from South Asia,"* he explains. *"It was not a social or cultural norm that they would see me as their boss."* He realized that these assumptions couldn't be changed through the exercising of autocratic power. He decided to engage with the team's present "knowing" and to challenge it by making the assumptions explicit and building rapport with people on a one-on-one basis.

Employed proactively, doubt can help us challenge our assumptions and beliefs, and bring a more nuanced grey into a world of black and white polarizations. Seeing alternative options can free us up from the constraints of the well-trodden path and open up new opportunities that were previously unseen. The key skill is to notice when we make an assumption, to recognize the assumption and 'suspend' it, just long enough to ask questions. This 'suspension' of judgement temporarily is called "bracketing." Rather than make assumptions, we stay open to what is said and ask more questions.

Gestalt practitioner Phil Joyce and psychotherapist Charlotte Sills give the example of a situation where somebody gets a promotion.[80] We might be tempted to say: *"Congratulations, that must be wonderful."* Yet if we bracketed this for a moment and asked them how they felt about it, we might get a surprising reply *"It's awful, my manager resigned and now I have double the workload without extra pay."* Or alternatively if a colleague says: *"I lost my job,"* we might be tempted to commiserate. Yet if we enquired *"how is that for you?"* we might be told: *"I have wanted to resign for a very long time, it's just the push that I needed."*

6.
CHALLENGE AUTHORITY AND EXPERTISE

*"Our freedom to doubt was born
of a struggle against authority in the
early days of science. It was a very deep
and strong struggle."*

Physicist Richard Feynman

We began the first chapter in this book with the story of Vesalius (see page 36), to whom we now return. The year 1537 was one of rich learnings for Vesalius, who fast-tracked his studies and completed his medical degree in less than 12 months. Shortly after his graduation he was appointed professor of surgery and anatomy at only 23 years of age. In this new role Vesalius was able to spend most of his time focusing on what he loved most – dissecting and exploring in great detail all parts of the human body. Records of notes he made of his first public dissection in December 1537 provide a great insight into his groundbreaking approach and signal the beginning of what later became his challenge of Galenism.

For the first time in the University of Padua's history, a medical professor broke with tradition. Vesalius stepped down from his throne, took a scalpel in his own hands, dispensed with both the surgeon and the demonstrator, and started cutting into the body of an 18-year-old male. As was the custom of the day, he first opened the abdominal cavity, then the thorax, moving on to the head and neck, then the brain and lastly the extremities.[90] At some point he used a dissected dog for comparative purposes, which later became his teaching trademark. The most striking thing about this dissection, though, was not Vesalius' willingness to get his hands dirty, literally, but his decision to use his own observations during the process and form his own judgements, rather than rely solely on Galen's texts. His notes are a record of his detailed observations and his approach during the dissection: *"I gave careful consideration to the possibility that anatomical dissection might be used to check speculation."*[81]

Vesalius' first dissection at the University of Padua marks the beginning of an extraordinary career. It was then that the seeds were sown for his core philosophy, which would shape the course of modern anatomy – that is, to refuse to accept past authority until his own research and studies had proved it true.[82] Over the coming years his dissections came to be seen as the most extensive anatomical investigations of his time. His research exposed more and more mistakes by Galen and consolidated the view that Galen was not infallible. He noted *"The descriptions of Galen ... are not always consistent."*[83] Vesalius discovered many discrepancies, including the fact that the human breastbone was made of three segments rather than seven as Galen had claimed, and that the humerus (the upper arm bone) was not the second-longest bone in the body but the fourth. He was no longer a faithful follower of Galen's entrenched authority.

Vesalius' groundbreaking work drew admiration from students and scholars alike, but the staunch Galenists of the time criticized him for his disobedience, seeing him as a mere dissector with a scalpel. Whilst he would regularly draw over a hundred people, mostly young students, to his public dissections, the more conservative members of the audience would often walk out in disgust at his pedagogical techniques.[84] Vesalius' biggest breakthrough came when he realized that Galen had not based his findings on the dissection of human bodies, but on those of monkeys, pigs and goats. As human dissections were illegal during Roman times, Galen had had to resort to dissecting animals to learn about the human body.

It only took Vesalius two years to launch a full challenge to Galen's work. To show students how wrong Galen had been, he gave lectures in which he compared skeletons of humans with those of animals, illustrating the discrepancies. He gave students the opportunity to test Galen's claims by using their own observations and forming their own judgements about the human body. He spent the next four years developing an extensive anatomy book based on his own studies and discoveries. He called it *De humani corporis fabrica libri septem*, or *The Seven Books on the Structure of the Human Body*, commonly known as *The Fabrica*. Published in 1543, *Fabrica* fully severed with the bonds of Galenic tradition and launched Vesalius' pioneering approach in anatomy based on independent observation and exploration.

Vesalius set a new course for the medical profession and influenced the work of countless scientists to come after him, including Darwin's evolutionary theory 300 years later. Padua became the most famous anatomical theatre in Europe and the university is to this day recognized for its freedom of thought in study and teaching.

Vesalius had to close his eyes to existing knowledge to be able to see something new. Sometimes we need to put aside the existing agreed knowledge. We need to challenge the presumptions of knowledge people have taken to be truth over time. This deliberate "putting aside" of the existing agreed knowledge enables exploration "as if" there was no current knowledge. This enables discovery and challenging what we thought was truth but in fact was just a "truth in time," a view seen to be true at a point in time.

English author and economist Noreena Hertz in her TED talk on "democratizing expertise" urges us to be ready and willing to challenge experts, to question the evidence, the assumptions and the potential omissions. She advocates creating a space for managed dissent, where expert ideas are aired and debated. This necessitates an environment where knowledge from divergent, discorded and heretical views is not only allowed, but encouraged; where the focus is not on displaying our expertise, but on wrestling with the most challenging issues at hand.

7.

QUESTION

"If I had an hour to solve a problem and my life depended on the answer, I would spend the first 55 minutes figuring out the proper questions to ask. For if I knew the proper questions, I could solve the problem in less than five minutes."

Albert Einstein

Steven: *I remember a meeting with a Zen master in North London. Master Ja An (or Bogumila Malinowska, her Polish name) is a slight woman with brown mousy hair. She opened the door to the Zen Centre, which is also where she lives, greeting me with a warm welcome. In the corridor I almost tripped over a bike and there seemed to be lots of shoes. "My son's," she explained, catching the bike and preventing it from falling on me. "Even Zen masters who live with teenagers can have clutter," I thought with some form of relief. It all seemed so ordinary. Before I knocked I was anticipating how a Zen master would act. I was not expecting her to be out of breath, just having returned from another errand. "Please make yourself welcome," as she showed me to the Dharma room. It looked like a living room that had a clear wooden floor and two rows of cushions, leading to one end of a statue of the Buddha. One side of the room was a window with a panoramic view over North London. Above the kitchen door I noticed a picture of the lineage of Zen masters to the Kwan Um school of Zen. To the right was Zen master Seung Sahn who had brought Zen to the West.*

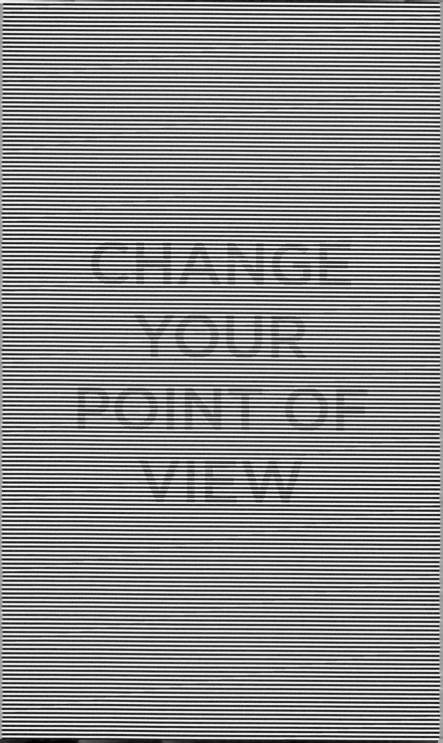

"What is the essence of Zen?" I asked. She answered: "Letting myself experience....Don't Know. Being myself and not pretending to be anyone else. You need to understand that this is a process, a never-ending process. Moment by moment we have to learn anew, we have to be very aware and present, without any opinion or judgment about ourselves or others."

I liked the idea of teaching not being words but essentially the way of being. Yet I knew that in Zen, the way to reach this state was often by using words to go beyond words, through a koan. Koans are literally statements that the student chews over. I knew of the famous koan 'what is the sound of one hand clapping?' So I asked Master Ja An "Do you remember your first koan?" She looked deep in thought, trying to recall. Probably because she had so many throughout the years. In the Zen tradition there are meant to be more than 1,300 koans.

"Why is the sky blue? was my first koan, given in an interview with other students and Zen Master Seung Sahn. With koans you can always go deeper. They are not about finding an answer, but rather coming to explore how this koan is working in your life. Some people due to the Western way of learning find it very difficult to accept that it is not about the answer. People want to achieve something, get a certificate or get recognition. They always ask 'how much practice should I do to become enlightened?', 'how long will it take me to become a master?' The shift from an intellectual inquiry to an intuitive inquiry is very difficult for them. I remember before I got my first koan my master said 'you must hit the floor'. I didn't know why he was asking me this but I hit the floor. Now, people need to know 'why' they do things. People want to achieve, to have an answer. Normally the way we get answers in life is like a collector. Zen is more about digestion of the answer." She asked me if I would like to try a koan.

I put my notebook down. Suddenly I became very self-conscious. I was no longer the scribe, the observer, but would be the student. Master Ja An picked up a small wooden stick, and looked me in *the eye. "Zen means understanding yourself. What is your name?" Suddenly I felt anxious and my breathing became shallow, with a mild panic. I was taken back to an interview scene where I had to get the right answer. Normally the questions in that case were intellectual and I could give a similarly intellectual answer in response.*

The simplicity of this question "What is your name?" disarmed me. I sat in silence for a few seconds, not knowing how to respond. "Well, my name is Steven" I replied. "I did not ask for your given name," Master Ja An responded firmly. "What is your name?" she asked again. My anxiety was increasing now. Master Ja An repeated the question, this time gently. "What is your name?" Time seemed to stop. I felt totally stupid, not being able to tell her my name. I said: "Well, I could say it is nothing or I could say it is something." And she replied: "If you say it is nothing I will hit you 30 times symbolically with this stick. If you say it is something I will still hit you with the stick 30 times."

I got the impression that if I had not been in London in 2012 she would have used the stick rather than talk about it symbolically. Seeing I was struggling, she gave me a passage to read. It described how the clouds come and go and they do not exist. Again she asked "What is your name?" "I honestly don't know how to answer," I replied.

Suddenly she slapped her hand on the ground, making a sharp noise. It was wordless. Asking the question "What is your name?" was not an attempt to help me find an answer, but to experience that moment of Not Knowing. I heard her hand slap the ground. There was a break from my thinking. Instead, a wordless space. Any word I used to describe it, even 'emptiness', would be a lie, putting something into the wordless. At this point, I realized I had drunk none of the tea. Suddenly we looked at the time and it was time for Master Ja An's driving lesson. I gave my thanks to the master and saw myself out while the Zen master quickly transformed into the driving lesson student.

Martine Batchelor, a Zen teacher who spent 10 years as a Zen nun in Korea, encourages us to become at one with the question. Developing a practice of questioning, rather than answering, means focusing on the question mark, not the meaning of the words. This allows us to create an openness to the present moment, letting go of our need for knowledge and security.[85]

Asking questions we already know the answer to only reinforces what we know – it provides instant gratification. If we don't already know the answer, we have the tendency to accept the first one that is generated. Keeping the questions going rather than settling on the first answer disturbs the equilibrium, is uncomfortable, and is generally not rewarded in our workplaces. The higher the confusion and uncertainty, the more attractive the answers become. Staying with the questions develops our tolerance and increases our capacity to engage with the unknown. It also provides us with more information about what is going on and what our options may be.

Eurostar is the operator of the high-speed rail line that runs under the English Channel between France and Britain. It is a complex business with many unknowns, such as the comparative cost of airline seats (key competitors to Eurostar), staff and operational costs, future unknown competitors, and the rise of substitutes for travel such as videoconferencing. Steven had worked with the CEO Nicolas Petrovic and his management team. Nicolas describes the challenge of fostering a culture that values questions as much as answers.

"When you go down the line from the top, most senior managers and middle managers are experts. They have credibility in knowing their stuff. Sometimes I find they put too much emphasis on the detail, buzzwords, spreadsheets. Part of creating a culture of Not Knowing is encouraging them to step back out of the detail and instead to sense check themselves and their decisions. For example, to ask 'Would I do this with my own money?', 'If I was the customer, would I like it?'"

We can foster an orientation towards questioning in ourselves and our workplaces by approaching, with curiosity, other views and opinions, being open to differences and multiple possibilities, and creating the arena for sharing dilemmas and doubts. We can choose to reward curiosity and questioning rather than reinforce dependency on answers.

LEAP IN THE DARK

CHAPTER 8

"Living is a form of not being sure, not knowing what next or how. The moment you know how, you begin to die a little. The artist never entirely knows. We guess. We may be wrong, but we take leap after leap in the dark."

American dancer and choreographer Agnes de Mille

1.

IMPROVISE

Leading change and leading others is an improvisational process, like playing jazz. It requires us to be fully present to deal with the unpredictability of the situation. It means being open to the possibility inherent in every moment and being prepared to let go of the plan.

Improvise comes from the Latin *improvisus* which means "not seen ahead of time." Improvisers approach life with a sense of play, engaging in something because they like it, for the joy of it. They are open and receptive to the offer. As Alex Sangster, an actor with the Playback Theatre Company in Melbourne, explains: *"If someone throws a ball at you and you catch it, that's when the game starts. The game is on and something magic can happen... If you are not fully present, you are not fully open to the offer. The possibility is not there and able to be realized. To sit in Not Knowing is unbelievably liberating and exciting."*

Alex often comes across a common misconception about improvisation – that it means to make things up on the spot. In fact, improvising starts with knowing the structure. Just like a great jazz musician, we first need to know the patterns and rituals within the process to be able to let go of them and improvise.

The structure helps set the boundaries and creates the space for experimentation and the creative process to take place. Once we know the rules, we are then able to throw away the plan and work away from the score, *"to let the river move where it's supposed to move,"* according to jazz pianist Keith Jarrett.

For filmmaker Anna Beckmann it is the technical combined with the mysterious that makes great films. *"The Not Knowing aspect of the filmmaking process is one of the most exciting and potentially fruitful elements of the process,"* she argues.

Anna gives the example of Ingmar Bergman, a prolific Swedish filmmaker for whom writing and directing were primarily uncertain and unconscious processes. He is known to have admitted that most of his conscious efforts had ended in embarrassing failure. Other filmmakers see the uncertain and mysterious element as a way of connecting the heart and the mind, a process which Anna believes is essential to almost every artistic process. *"It is this tension between heart and mind and the paradox of mystery and familiarity which I think drives most good films. We are intrigued by unknown situations, characters and locations, but something culturally or universally relevant keeps us relating as we are taken on the finely crafted cinematic journey."*

Anna describes the process Ingmar Bergman went through when he made his films, working very delicately at the edge between the structure of certainty and the creative elements of chaos and uncertainty. *"He began his script-writing process by grappling with some uncertain or unknown aspect within himself, which he would then try to resolve or explore through characterization and narrative."*

Ingmar Bergman described the script-making process as a collaboration between intuition and intellect: *"I throw a spear into the darkness. That is intuition. Then I must send an army into the darkness to find the spear. That is intellect."*

Bergman used the final, "watertight" script and the technical element of the production as a foundation for improvisation. He was both in control of what could be controlled and open and ready to enter into uncertain territory with his actors, allowing for unpredictable spontaneous elements to arise, helping create what Anna calls *"the ineffable magic that pulses through his work."*

Taking the improvisational process further, contemporary director and writer Mike Leigh fully embraces uncertainty in his filmmaking process. When watching Leigh's films it is often clear that he and his actors go into the process without a definite idea about what will be created. This contributes to the deeply realistic feel of his films, which reflect the uncertain quality of our real everyday lives. *"He begins with the kernel of an idea which he then, using improvisational process, begins to work with over with his actors for months and months, fleshing out the story and subtleties of the characters until the film, a genuine act of exploration for its creator, its actors, and its viewers, is finally made,"* says Anna.

Multi-disciplinary artist, facilitator and theatre-maker Raisa Breslava took an intuitive leap into Not Knowing when she embarked on a journey of directing a theatre production, which came to be known as "WIMP." It was a one-man show performed by Vincent Manna in London, September 2013. Never having directed a play for theatre or worked with an actor before, it was an intimate experience of improvisation for Raisa. She had not received any training in theatre directing, nor had she worked with actors before. Without further training she decided to learn about the discipline through direct practice.

"I dived into the void. I found a performer who was interested in collaborating with me and so we began. There is no universally accepted manual on how to work with an actor, nor is there a manual on how to make art, you just start and find out by doing it, so I did. It was terrifying and exciting – what do I do? How do I do it? I was no director, I was just a woman in a room with a man. A woman who wanted to passionately create through the medium of theatre."

Raisa knew one thing for certain – that she was creating work that was based on the performer himself. The artist was the content of the work. His ability to be vulnerable and connect with the audience through that vulnerability became the anchor that enabled Raisa to trust the unknown. Rather than panic, she would work in rehearsals with whatever was happening that day. *"If the actor was feeling quite rigid, agitated and stuck, I looked for ways to include that stuckness, not push it away, not create techniques that would dissolve it, or push the actor beyond it. I used the stuckness as the art material itself."*

She would sometimes arrive at the sessions and have nothing prepared, no plan. *"I would walk into the space, the actor would arrive. These first moments before a rehearsal begins are filled with the unknown. Any part of me that feared this void would hate to be here. I wanted to escape, not trust, and any self-hating/ self-limiting beliefs would be evident in this short time-scale of the unknown."*

What guided Raisa was her deep faith and trust in the process. She kept going with what felt organic and let the process evolve naturally, without prescribing a limited, controlled vision of an end-product.

Raisa was also guided by the way in which she took up her role of director. She didn't adopt preconceived, presupposed, ex-pected ways of playing this role out. She wanted to tease the role out through getting to know herself and through the co-creation with the actor. *"I wanted the process to show me what worked and what didn't. So as far as the roles went, I saw my main job as guiding, holding and being a container for the process, and lead-ing the actor into deeper, more authentic, and powerful depths."*

For Raisa, when we approach each moment as new, without the nonchalance that can come from perceived familiarity, a new relationship opens up to the present, one of unmediated experi-ence and intimacy.

We can find new ways of taking up our roles and working with others in ways that bring out our creativity and spon-taneity. We can tap into the potential of Not Knowing by throwing a spear into the darkness as an advance exploration party, then follow the process by deploying the technical skill and expertise required to refine, tighten and bring to life the intuitive leap.

2.
GENERATE MULTIPLE HYPOTHESES

*"Watson, you can see everything.
You fail, however, to reason from what
you see. You are too timid in drawing
your inferences."*

Sherlock Holmes
The Adventure of the Blue Carbuncle (1892)

Sir Arthur Conan Doyle's fictional detective Sherlock Holmes is famous for his methodical approach to solving criminal mysteries. Hypotheses play a central role in Holmes' cases as they guide his investigations. In the *Hound of the Baskervilles*, Holmes is investigating how Sir Charles Baskerville died. Once he carefully observes the corpse, he develops two hypotheses: he was either attacked by a dog or died of a heart attack. Holmes collects data by scanning the surrounding environment. He mysteriously spends time alone in a cave and visits the nearby village. From the new evidence he develops a further hypothesis – that Stapleton killed Sir Charles to get hold of his fortune. To test this hypothesis he sets up a risky experiment, provoking Stapleton to release his hound to attack the younger Baskerville. You'll have to read the book to find out what happens next.

Holmes formulated hypotheses by interpreting the facts but never accepted his first hypothesis as being the truth. He kept on revising his hypotheses in light of new available data, and was able to hold multiple perspectives without being overly attached to any one. In a way, Holmes demonstrated a case of "beginner's mind" as he approached problems. He wasn't bound by his previous knowledge or cases. He learned from every tiny detail and remained open to the facts – even if they changed along the way.

Dr Thomas Bolte is a boyish-looking 51-year-old modern-day Sherlock Holmes. Based in New York, Bolte is a medical detective specializing in solving medical mysteries. He calls himself a "comprehensivist," a diagnostician who steps beyond mainstream medicine to solve an evasive health issue.[86] Others have described him as a "zebra hunter," someone who looks for the zebra when he hears hooves, while everyone else is looking for the horse. He is renowned for diagnosing the undiagnosable, picking up cases that haven't been solved by other doctors, with an astonishing 95% rate of success.

Bolte embodies Holmes' ability to formulate and weigh different and competing explanations of the evidence. People comment about Bolte's ability to look at every situation from a new perspective, looking for what others may have missed in unlikely places where nobody has previously looked, asking questions that haven't been asked. In Bolte's words *"my life is so kooky crazy, nothing surprises me."*

In the business world, we often devalue diagnosis because we're generally rewarded for leaping to action. However, when we are facing the unknown, a pre-existing solution orientation does not serve us well. Instead, we need to be deliberate in creating a space of possibility, a conscious assessment of what's going on and what's possible through a process of diagnosis – observing and collecting data and making a series of interpretations, which Holmes and Bolte are now famous for.

Intuit Inc, the creator of tax software Quicken, is a rare breed of company that champions leadership by experiment and decision-making by hypothesis.[87] Scott Cook, the founder of Intuit, explains that instead of being guided by the opinion of the boss in decision-making, as is usually the case, the emphasis at Intuit is on getting people to make decisions based on their own hypotheses and experiments.[88]

The Intuit lean experiment loop starts with an idea, like Intuit India setting out to create new businesses that improve the financial lives of poor Indian farmers. Their vision was to raise farmers' incomes by 10%. Once the idea was articulated, the team set out to find an important, unsolved customer problem. They immersed themselves in the lives of the farmers to gain a deep understanding of the issue, a process Intuit calls "deep customer empathy."

One problem they discovered was that the farmers didn't know which market to take their produce to in order to get the highest price. This seemed to be a good opportunity for Intuit, who thought that they could build a system where they could text farmers today's best wholesale prices and which market agent was offering them. However, unlike many companies who would at this point go ahead and implement the "solution," Intuit has added a few more steps to their process.

Next comes the "leap of faith," where the team comes up with a series of hypotheses. In the Indian farmers' example, the team's hypotheses to be tested included:

• Enough market agents will share the prices with Intuit
• Market agents will honour the prices they give
• Typically illiterate farmers can read SMS
• Farmers will change behaviour based on SMS
• Farmers will perceive that they acquired a better price
• Intuit can monetize the opportunity
• Revenue will exceed cost[89]

Cook explains that seven weeks after discovering this opportunity and developing the hypothesis, the Indians started testing their hypotheses and running a series of experiments, including:

• pilot test of 15 farms
• data collection tests
• farmer acquisition tests
• push versus pull messaging tests
• alternate crop test
• price test
• advertising tests
• outsource sales test

The experiments drove the decision-making so that when they started delivering to farmers the prices at their local wholesale options on a simple mobile phone, they found out the method worked. After 13 more experiments, the results showed that farmers reported a 20% improvement in their farm income. Cook explains: *"Now, for a poor farmer, for many of them, it's the difference between their children going to school and not going to school. Yet this is a business that the bosses, including myself, would have said no to."*[90]

Sherlock Holmes always started with a dead body. Since he didn't know the cause of the death, he generated a range of hypotheses about it, even ones that seemed unlikely. When new information came up, he applied it to the case and adjusted it as he went along. Hypothesizing prevented Holmes from jumping to conclusions too soon, which, as we've seen earlier (see part I), is what we tend to do, to bad effect, when we come to the edge of what we know.

The Intuit example shows how a company can adopt a Not Knowing approach when they enter a new market and test a new product. By setting up a business system that requires clear articulation of hypotheses, employees can move into the unknown with confidence because they have internalized the acceptance of the unknown. A culture has been built up that depoliticizes the process of forming views about the future (e.g. "this will be a good market"). In most organizations, people put forward a view and then spend their energy advocating it, to the detriment of the learning process. These are provisional ideas, best guesses, tentative explanations rather than fixed answers or solutions. When we feel we have to advocate for a position, we have a vested interest in proving it is right. The beauty of hypotheses is that no one needs to have a vested interest in the answer. Instead of becoming a champion for one possible explanation or model, the interest of the group is in collecting as many as possible and proving or disproving them. The focus is on discovery and revision, on considering all hypotheses plausible until new evidence is found that causes us to rule one of the hypotheses out.

However, many of us don't work in an environment like this. Faced with tremendous pressure to deliver results, and fast, it may prove challenging to take the time to hold and play with multiple interpretations and perspectives on an issue. Providing alternative frames for looking at problems rather than solutions may frustrate, even infuriate, those who are expecting us to come up with a quick answer. It takes courage to be interpretative.

3.
BRING DIVERSE VOICES TOGETHER

Founded in 1925 by Alexander Graham Bell, Bell Laboratories is perhaps one of the most famous technology innovation companies in the world, known for developing revolutionary radio astronomy, the transistor, the laser, and the UNIX operating system among many others. Seven Nobel Prizes have been awarded for work associated with Bell Labs. Deb Mills-Scofield, a strategy and innovation consultant, who started her career at Bell Labs, describes her experience working in an environment that encouraged hypothesis formation and testing.

"My entire career at Bell Labs and AT&T was a continuous journey of Not Knowing and discovery – that was our business. At Bell Labs, Not Knowing meant that I might have a question like 'why does/doesn't this work this way?' and be allowed to go figure out why. Not Knowing started with either a question for which you had no hypothesis or a question for which you had a hypothesis or two and were ready to go test. You didn't know what the answer was – you didn't know the outcome, either precisely or even at all. The goal was to find out."

The culture at Bell Labs thrived on cross-disciplinary collaboration. Deb could chat with physicists, psychologists, economists, computer scientists, mechanics, and electrical engineers, amongst many others.

"The building where I worked was specifically designed for random collisions of people from different backgrounds, with long sunny corridors and atria for hanging out to chat or just work instead of in your own office. I could create more questions, hypotheses, and experimental designs by walking the trails around the building, sitting out in the sun by the big ponds, or by going down

to the ocean a few minutes away. I could listen to music in my office or while I stayed home in my PJs all day to work. Many times, I'd go to museums or galleries to get my design ideas flowing. I didn't have, nor was I expected, to stay within the four walls of my office or my building."

Working across difference is the foundation for innovation and creativity; it is also a key ingredient for making progress on complex challenges where there is a diversity of views about what the challenge is and what needs to be done in order to move forwards. Engaging with others in dialogue becomes a necessary step on the journey into the unknown.

In contrast with conversation, in which people exchange existing ideas, and perhaps advocate their own point of view, the process of dialogue involves a "suspension" of sorts. Allowing time to take in what the other person is saying, without having a prepared answer. In this deep listening there is a space in which a different response than the usual, habitual pattern or routine becomes available. A space where a deeper level of conversation can take place. Agreement might not be reached, but empathy and respect are conditions to allow this to manifest. When true dialogue takes place, the bitterest of enemies can sit together and hear each other.

Danny Gal is a young Israeli man who in the midst of the biggest social protests in his country decided to harness the power of dialogue among diverse ethnic, political and social groups for social change.

He remarks: *"We are in a period of change and the public can no longer be ignored. Decision-makers today can't continue to ignore what people are demanding and no leader can just assume that he knows what the people want."* This also holds true for organizations. Each of us, no matter what level or role, can help create the conditions for dialogue. Danny was no political leader but he stepped up to do what was needed.

The catalyst for Danny's mission was an event he organised that brought together Israelis and Palestinians, sitting together in a circle. After a while a young man spoke softly: *"I am a Palestinian from a village. I was an ambulance driver and now I'm working with youth in danger on the streets. I'm here because my brother was a suicide bomber and killed himself and 17 Israeli civilians. I want to prevent other tragic events like that."* Later, when the participants were asked to pair up, Danny made his way over to the young man, compelled to hear more of his story. *"My brother saw his best friend shot and killed at school by Israelis. This filled him with anger and the desire for revenge. He fell into a crowd of people that took him in the wrong direction."* That moment Danny realized the power of dialogue and bringing diverse voices together.

With little more than an idea of connecting people, Danny formed his first NGO The Centre for Emerging Futures. His purpose was to build trust between people as human beings and not as representatives of their communities. The hope was that they would share their humanity and acknowledge the pain and suffering on both sides.

In the summer of 2011 the Arab Spring began and the Middle East saw a wave of protests from Cairo to Libya to Tunisia. Thousands protested for basic rights to education and employment and a greater say in their government. The same happened that summer in Israel. People were discontent with the high cost of living, the growing inequality and the lack of political leadership. This took the form of street protests when one young woman, Daphni Leef, set up a tent in the streets of Tel Aviv as an act of civil disobedience to raise public attention to the issues. Soon, through social media and online campaigns, hundreds of people joined her. There were hundreds of tents and in one week that summer half a million Israelis marched in the streets calling out for "Social Justice" and reforms in Netanyahu's government. Danny saw these events as an opportunity to take the movement beyond protest to a form of reconciliation.

On Saturday 10 September 2011 Danny ran the biggest civic dialogue in Israel. Over 10,000 people – Arabs, Jews, Orthodox Jews, new immigrants from Russia and Ethiopia, settlers, lefties and right-wingers from more than 30 cities across Israel – sat together and participated in a dialogue.

Like his previous work on dialogue between Palestinians and Israelis, respect was set as a ground rule and everybody shared who they were, and why they chose to come to the event. A thousand round tables were brought in to symbolise equality for participants. Hundreds of volunteer facilitators kept the focus on appreciative questions such as 'what is one thing that you want to change and you are willing to take responsibility for?' The media reported some of the highlights of the dialogues and these were fed back to government to influence policy so people could see their voice was being heard. But mostly it was the act in itself – sitting down together with strangers – that was the main achievement that evening.

Danny reflects on his feelings that night:

"Not Knowing is like standing at the edge of a cliff and knowing that jumping is completely insane. You know that what has been happening has brought misery for people's lives. But moving to the new is a step into the unknown that risks everything. When you are there it is the voice of fear that stops you. I have learned to always listen to my body in these edge situations. I listen to my heart beat. I know that when my heart beats strongly it tells me I have to make the move. What is known is that we can't continue as in the past. We don't need to know the how, what or why of the future. I just need to make the step."

4.

TAKE MEANINGFUL RISK

*"And the day came when the risk
to remain tight in a bud was more painful
than the risk it took to blossom."*

Author Anaïs Nin

Author and travel writer Nick Thorpe was used to driving himself hard to meet deadlines and lead the life he wanted. However, as he approached midlife, the strain was beginning to tell. Used to writing about new destinations, Nick was bewildered and terrified one morning when a workaholic breakdown left him in unknown psychological territory.

"I was hunched at my desk as usual, feeling about as healthy as road kill, racing to meet a deadline, when suddenly I found I couldn't type another word," he remembers. *"My hands wouldn't do what I asked of them. It was a terrifying experience for someone who had always done everything through sheer effort – because it dawned on me at last that crude willpower doesn't last forever. It's a bit like oil. And mine had just run out."*

Even at the time, however, Nick's fear was mixed with something like relief as he struck out into an unknown territory.

"I basically surrendered, blew some deadlines, let some people down. If I was going to avoid a complete breakdown, I needed to stop bullying myself into action and risk trying another way."

Nick embarked on what he now recognizes as a spiritual quest. A quest to meet people and situations that could teach him how to stop holding on so fiercely to the certainties in his life. To let go a little. *"At the start I took it rather literally. I went cliff-jumping and free-falling on the wings of a biplane. I soon began to experiment with emotional and social ways to let go, including clowning, naturism, and various workshops which encouraged me to make myself much more vulnerable than I was comfortable being."*

Nick didn't know what the outcome of his risk-taking would be. Looking back, he considers this to be the richest and most transformative year of his life. He learned to trust life more and live in the present. He also took the momentous step of becoming an adoptive dad.

Nick reflects that he was able to take those risks because he had a baseline of safety from which to attempt them. Just as he could only give himself to wing-walking when he knew he had a reliable harness, or try naturism when he knew there was a code that nobody would point or joke, so he realized that his son could only grow when he truly knew that he was safely parented.

Nick admits there are days when risk-taking seems like a big stretch. *"I see it in my eight-year-old son, who is like most of us, deep down. Some days we're safety seekers, other days we're risk takers, trusting ourselves enough to push boundaries like healthy growing children and see what happens. But what if even our mistakes, our so-called failings, our times of Not Knowing, are simply part of growth?"* he asks. *"I've noticed that when I can believe that, I lose my fear, and I'm open to almost anything."*

The fears and anxieties experienced at the edge may be well founded because the unknown can be a scary place, where our identity, comfort and wellbeing are at risk. The decision to proceed cannot be taken lightly. Each one of us must assess the context within which we operate, what the situation is calling for, our own level of tolerance, and the support available to us to ascertain the level of risk we are prepared to take.

5.
EXPLORE

"One doesn't discover new lands without consenting to lose sight of the shore for a very long time."

French author André Gide

In May 2012 cult legend John Waters, the writer and director of iconic movies *Polyester* and *Hairspray*, otherwise known as the "Pope of Trash," embarked on an eight-day hitchhiking journey across the US from his hometown of Baltimore to San Francisco. Sporting his iconic pencil-thin moustache and a cardboard sign that read "I'm Not Psycho," he braved lonely roads and put his life in the hands of strangers to take him to the final destination. The story, which eventually was published in a book titled *Carsick*, might as well be the screenplay for one of his movies.

Among his 15 rides he met an 81-year-old farmer, a married couple from Illinois, then a young councilman and Republican picked him up in his Corvette in pouring rain. Convinced he was homeless and feeling sorry for Waters, he drove him four hours from Maryland to Ohio. By then he was so taken with Waters that he reconnected with him in Denver, Colorado, to drive him 1,600 km and 22 hours to Reno, Nevada, then met up with him again in San Francisco to stay at his apartment.[91]

Indie rock band *Here We Go Magic*, from Brooklyn, who were on tour, eventually picked him up on a stretch of Interstate 70 in Ohio. They couldn't believe their eyes when they spotted him by an exit ramp, sporting a hat that said "Scum of the Earth."[92]

In an interview with the New York Times Waters commented that he was driven by a need to "give himself up to the winds" and surrender. *"My life is so over-scheduled,"* he said, *"what will happen if I give up control?"*[93] The surprising lesson was that *"it can sometimes be thrilling to not know where life is taking you."*

Australian sea and ice adventurer Chris Bray, a 28-year-old Australian Geographic young adventurer of the year in 2012, shares Waters' appetite for new experiences.

"There's something pretty special about doing something, or going somewhere, that no human ever has ... Then, not only is it a new experience for me personally, which makes everyone feel more alert and alive, but knowing I'm the 'first' adds this overarching feeling of awe in realizing that anything could happen next.... It's that uncertainty, that stepping into the unknown, that pulls the entire experience into a whole new level of focus, heightens all my senses and demands me to live completely in the present. It's an unforgettable privilege to experience."[94]

Not Knowing is the frisson that makes life worth living. Imagine that we woke up every morning at exactly the same time, to the same conditions, met the same people and had the same challenges and opportunities. The concept was explored in the comedy *Groundhog Day* where the comedian Bill Murray, who plays Phil Connors, a meteorologist, starts to relive one day again and again. While at first he can take advantage of knowing what people will do, and has fun seducing women and breaking the law, eventually he becomes anxious, bored and irritated. He cannot even kill himself, waking up each morning as in a time loop to the same tune on the radio.

Even in a predictable world Phil's stumbling block is a relationship with someone he cannot control. He ultimately realizes that his ability to use his prior knowledge to manipulate her leaves him dissatisfied and fails to win her over. Even though the circumstances of the day may be known, he decides to recreate his own day, learning new skills such as ice sculpting and piano, and steps into the unknown.

6.

EXPERIMENT

Franklin D Roosevelt's (FDR's) iconic words delivered on Sunday 22 May 1932 at a commencement address for the graduates of Oglethorpe University are still reverberating through the American political landscape: *"The country needs and, unless I mistake its temper, the country demands bold, persistent experimentation. It is common sense to take a method and try it: If it fails, admit it frankly and try another. But above all, try something."*[95]

Eighty years later, at the 2012 Democratic National Convention, President Barack Obama invoked them to argue that: *"It will take more than a few years for us to solve challenges that have built up over decades. It will require common effort, shared responsibility, and the kind of bold, persistent experimentation that Franklin Roosevelt pursued during the only crisis worse than this one."*[96]

Both FDR and Obama's speeches provoked negative reactions from critics on both sides of the political divide. The then New York governor, FDR was criticized by the *New York Times* about his blandness and lack of specificity, whilst his own advisor, Louis Howe, called it an appalling piece of stupidity.[97] History now shows that FDR's Oglethorpe speech was a turning point in his career, marking the beginning of an experimental approach to tackling the Great Depression of the 1930s, and the implementation of the New Deal, a series of programmes passed during his first term. With this experimental approach FDR was known to sometimes put forward multiple projects, some at cross-purposes, exasperating his staff and advisors.

It is not common for political leaders to talk of experimentation, let alone act on it. One leader who has quietly taken on one of the world's most complex challenges, drugs, is President of Uruguay José Mujica. At the end of 2013 he passed a law decriminalizing marijuana, calling it "an experiment."

This story is significant because it is so rare. While social scientists have run experiments about the effects of the decriminalization of drugs, it is a rare government that actually makes this a reality. No national government has decriminalized marijuana – Uruguay is the first – a test case for Latin America. The goal is to declare the "war on drugs" a failure, and try something else. To undermine the business model of drug cartels and upend the violence and destruction this brings.

It perhaps is no coincidence that Mujica is also famous for his frugal, modest lifestyle, donating 90% of his salary to charity. The notion that he is the world's poorest president has gone viral across the blogosphere. He is known as a philosopher, a true progressive. Guided by a strong purpose, Mujica has dared to venture into unknown territory in spite of strong opposition from many.

Mujica accepts the risks associated with such a daring experiment, and is prepared to change course if necessary: *"Like any experiment, naturally, there are risks, and we have to understand that if they prove too much for us, then we must backtrack. We do not have to be fanatics."*

Resistance is a common initial reaction in the face of experimentation, especially from risk-averse quarters. When Peter King suggested to the management team of Energeticos to throw away the organization chart (see page 172), it was greeted with astonishment. How would they be able to manage their reports if they didn't know who reported to them? Their resistance increased when Peter made another outrageous suggestion – do away with roles and responsibilities. After several hours of debating the pros and cons, Peter suggested that they "give it a try for three months." This became the trademark of the Energeticos change process. Experimentation became the best way to change paradigms and help people believe in new management practices.

"Experimentation is the ability to release ourselves from wanting to control a process, or expecting a particular outcome." There is no "one" way in experimentation, but a multitude of ways that can be tested to address the problem at hand. Organizations are generally risk-averse and not patient enough to experiment. The investment relies on delivering results, quickly, that don't cause any pain or cost any money. However, research shows that organizations that encourage experimentation are likely to be more innovative and successful than those that do not have this mindset, and teams that experiment frequently outperform those who don't.[98]

Eurostar is known for its openness to trial ideas. This happens in a limited scope because making a small change can sometimes be a big challenge with so many staff, passengers and procedures involved to make everything operate well (see also page 236). So rather than concentrate on making big changes, staff are encouraged to think of one small thing that they can try over a period of a few months. For example, Eurostar decided to offer taxi bookings on board the train for business-class customers. This idea was very well received and is now a regular service. CEO Nicolas Petrovic explains:

"When we first had the idea, we had the vision but none of the logistics in place to make it happen. 'It will never work', I was told by many. Yet we trialled it. We made many changes and improvements learning along the way till we got it right. Often people are not used to learning by trial and experimentation, including failure. They want the solution to come first. To make a culture of experimentation it's essential to get the line managers on board first. They need to be convinced you will not stop halfway and

give up, because it is their credibility on the line. There is nothing worse than starting and not finishing, so we learn continuously and make changes."

There are many advantages to fostering an orientation towards experimentation rather than towards problem-solving. An experimental mindset gives people the freedom to try things without feeling that everything is riding on their decisions and actions. A series of experiments can be run at the same time, which puts us in a situation where we have to pay close attention to what's working and what's not. The whole focus can then be on the learning derived from the experiments and the dissemination of the learnings.

Diana: A friend, Jane Harrison, likes to describe herself as a bowerbird, collecting bits of knowledge, experiences, relationships, just like the bowerbird collects brightly coloured objects in its nest. Jane is an artist, a playwright, an indigenous artist mentor, and a government policy officer, among other things. She calls herself "Jane of all trades." She is an anti-expert or what French anthropologist and ethnologist Lévi-Strauss calls a "bricoleur."

A bricoleur is the opposite of a specialist, an amateur who uses whatever is available at hand, like MacGyver from the show of the same name. MacGyver got himself out of tricky situations by putting together bits and pieces from seemingly disparate objects lying around, no matter what the problem was.

The bricoleur has an exploratory mindset, working at the edge between knowing and Not Knowing, constantly improvising and spontaneously engaging with the surrounding environment. For a bricoleur the process is as important as the end result.

7.
EMBRACE MISTAKES

*"Mistakes can take us to the margins,
to the unknown, the unexplored."*

John Caddell, The Mistake Bank

Geoff Mendal is an engineer at one of the leading internet companies in the world, based in California. He fits the
stereotype of a computer engineer – introverted, methodical
and structured. But he also loves food to the point that it is, at
times, an obsession. So he taught himself how to cook. Initially
he had no idea what he was doing and he made many mistakes.
With practice came competence, but cooking with competence
quickly became boring. *"What's the challenge in making the
same dish over and over again exactly the same way with the same
results? This is not to say that doing so is unimportant, quite the
contrary! Any restaurant chef will tell you that repeat customers
expect their dishes to taste exactly the same as when they ordered
them the last time, regardless of what is in season or the quality
of the ingredients available, or the team in the kitchen doing the
actual cooking."*

There are challenges to cooking the same dish the same way,
every time, says Geoff. It takes tremendous skill and competence

to be able to do so. *"This challenge is an emotional one. I know I can make a dish I have practised hundreds of times the same way as before and meet everyone's expectations, so why bother? There's nothing for me to learn or improve upon if I produce it the same way every time."*

When he decided to get really serious about cooking, Geoff went to a professional culinary school at night for a year's course. One night the class was preparing several different sauces at the same time. He mistakenly mixed up the ingredients of two of the sauces that he was prepping at his cooking station. By the time the instructor came around to observe his progress, it was too late. He pointed out Geoff's mistake but told him to continue preparing the mistaken sauces anyway. Maybe there was a lesson to be learned.

"I expected the results to be horrific, which for one of the sauces certainly was the case. But the other sauce – which I now call the 'Money Sauce' – turned out to be phenomenal. I took it home to let my wife taste it and it instantly became her favourite. She pleaded with me to make it again. But I could not, as I did not remember exactly the sequence of mistakes I made to produce it. I had only the recipes for the two sauces we were supposed to make, and though I tried to swap sets of ingredients and the processes for forming them, I could not duplicate my mistake, my 'Money Sauce'."

It took more than three years of experimentation to ascertain what the original mistakes were, but finally he succeeded. Now he can produce the phenomenal sauce he mistakenly made in culinary school that night every time.

Geoff admits that initially he approached cooking and culinary school using an engineering mindset: understand and follow the rules and the results will be great. Yet the culinary instructors told him that he would never be a great chef if he stuck to that approach. The challenge is to break free of the rules and become comfortable in a space where the recipe means little more than the starting point of an unknown journey. *"Cooking in the moment, being totally aware of what's happening right now and quickly adapting are what makes for great dishes. Letting go of the plan is not an easy task for an engineer. I'd hate to cross a bridge built by an engineer with this mindset. But for cooking, it's necessary and it works."*

Since graduating from culinary school, Geoff has befriended and worked with many professional chefs, usually for large catering or charity events. They are well respected and known in the industry for their great skill and delicious food and nice restaurants. Working with these chefs, Geoff has noticed that the menu plan is at best scribbled on a sheet of paper usually on the day of the event or the day before. Sometimes that plan is not provided to the team doing the cooking, rather only pieces of the plan are communicated verbally. For the most part, the team of chefs operates in a space of Not Knowing. The quantity and breadth of ingredients are well thought out – one cannot cook for hundreds of people at a lavish event without this kind of planning. But once the ordering is done, the process of actually producing the dishes is mostly in the moment. It is not uncommon to completely substitute a dish or prepare it in a way that is the opposite of how it was originally envisioned. Chefs constantly taste and adapt the dishes they are preparing. *"The best food is prepared in a fashion where not knowing how it will eventually be produced or taste rules the day,"* explains Geoff.

Geoff's ability to acknowledge and value the mistakes he made opened up possibilities that he could not have envisaged before. This is in contrast to the attitude in business where mistakes are often associated with failure and low performance. A study of US hospital nursing units showed that if mistakes are approached in the spirit of learning, then the opposite can be true. The study discovered a correlation between higher documented error rates and higher perceived unit performance, quality of relationships and nurse manager leadership. The primary reason for errors being detected in the first place in the unit was the staff's ability to discuss mistakes openly.[99]

At Eurostar, building a culture oriented towards learning from mistakes has been identified as a major opportunity. *"Perhaps the biggest learning is for people to accept mistakes. I find that people self-police themselves and are tougher on themselves and others than any corporate policy could be. We are working on creating an attitude of accepting mistakes and learning and growing from them, which is a key to effectiveness in Not Knowing,"* says CEO Nicolas Petrovic.

Prolific innovators are often very comfortable with mistakes. Thomas Edison reputedly said *"I make more mistakes than anyone I know. And eventually I patent them."* The car manufacturer Toyota is known for its efficiency and high-quality systems and is studied by manufacturers the world over. One of Toyota's systems is to hold regular meetings where people bring in their mistakes so that everyone can learn from them. The culture makes it safe for them to do so. As Neil Gershenfeld, director of the Massachusetts Institute of Technology's Centre for Bits and Atoms, says: *"Bugs are features – violations of expectations are opportunities to refine them."*

8.

FAIL FASTER

On 1 February 2003 the Columbia Space Shuttle disintegrated over Texas upon re-entry to the earth's atmosphere, killing all seven crew members. The direct cause of the disaster turned out to be a piece of foam dislodging and striking the exterior tiles, allowing hot gases to enter the body of the space shuttle when it re-entered the atmosphere. However, the disaster is also a well-known case study of organizational and group failure. Academics who studied the culture of NASA identified failures in group dynamics such as a lack of listening, learning and enquiring, and limited psychological safety for challenging authority. The culture relied on data-driven problem-solving and quantitative analysis, and discouraged new untried thinking and the exploration of incomplete yet troubling information.[100]

The problem wasn't failure itself, it was people's attitude to failure. They avoided looking at potential mistakes in order to avoid embarrassment and loss of self-confidence. They focused their energies on advocating their own or existing points of view, rather than staying open to the possibilities that something might be wrong with the existing system. It has been reported that even though they were concerned about the foam strike on the shuttle, NASA managers spent 17 days downplaying the possibility that this eventuality represented a serious problem, and therefore failed to look into the issue further.[101]

We measure our worthiness in terms of successes and achievements, wearing ambition like a badge of honour. We tend to have high expectations of ourselves and others, so that when we fail to achieve our goals, we feel disappointed. We tend to take credit when things succeed, and blame others when they don't. So failure often takes us by surprise. If "failure is not an option," we are thrown off course. We become depressed by our mistakes and see them as an affront to our self-worth, exposing our incompetence.

Our attitude to failure often seems to be cultural. People look to the dynamism of American entrepreneurial culture as epitomized by Silicon Valley and the startup world. Entrepreneurs are known to be proud of their failures, an attitude encapsulated in the motto of business startups: "fail faster." In some circles, if you haven't started a business and have not failed at least once, investors might not trust you. This experience and acceptance of failure is key to later success.

Contrast the puritan work ethic of the American East with the gold rush in the West which de-stigmatized failure. Whole populations tried digging and panning in random places both not knowing whether they would strike rich or where the gold was, seeing failure as a normal part of trying to become successful. As tens of thousands of people went through this process, the idea of failure gradually lost its sting. We can see the echoes of this in the modern entrepreneurial world of Silicon Valley, where having tried something and failed is not seen as a negative.

US design firm IDEO's core philosophy is "build to learn." Acting before having the answers, taking risks and fostering clumsiness are all encouraged and rewarded. One story tells of an employee who came back from his first-ever skiing trip and boasted in a meeting that he had skied for three days without ever falling down. Rather than being congratulated, he was derided for remaining within his comfort zone.[102]

Instead of avoiding the pain of failure, we could re-frame failure as vital feedback, an opportunity to learn. Just like self-guided cruise missiles, which constantly seek feedback and auto-correct themselves once launched, we can proactively seek feedback to enable us to take mid-course corrections. The very process of walking is one where we are constantly off balance and correct ourselves with each step we take, falling forwards. Entrepreneurs are adept at acknowledging the possibility of failure right from the beginning of a process, so that they can start considering all options, watching for the failure point, ready to adjust as they go along.

Rather than seeing failure as a source of shame and regret, we can view it as an acceptable and inevitable part of operating in a complex and uncertain environment. Not expecting to get it right the first time frees us up to get up and try again.

In a commencement speech to Harvard University, JK Rowling talked about failure as a *"stripping away of the inessential."* It allowed her to stop pretending to herself about who she was and start to focus her energy on what mattered most, her writing. *"I was set free, because my greatest fear had been realized,"* she explained. Had she succeeded at anything else, she might have never found the determination to succeed in writing. Sometimes we need to fail to realize what is important.

9.
WHY NOT?

I hear you say "Why?"
Always "Why?" You see things;
and you say "Why?"
But I dream things that never were;
and I say "Why not?"

Playwright George Bernard Shaw

Gordon D'Silva OBE founded the Hoxton Apprentice in 2003, a restaurant that trained hundreds of unemployed apprentices as chefs, waiters and bar staff. It was to be the model for UK celebrity chef Jamie Oliver's Fifteen restaurant. Gordon also launched "Training for Life," a social enterprise that raised several million pounds through social investments, fundraising and events. Its projects have returned over 17,000 people to work and full-time education.

Early in his career, while he was working for Dr Barnardo's children's charity, Gordon had to put a very vulnerable young person in accommodation in Earls Court, which at the time was synonymous with the sex trade. He says: *"I remember I was so upset. What we needed was an aftercare centre for those leaving care, but we had no money. This was Thatcher's England and budgets were slashed. Nothing existed in this space. I said to myself 'Fuck it, I will raise the money'."* Together with agencies and housing associations Gordon acquired an old

Victorian building and refurbished it. This became the first aftercare centre in the UK; a safe intermediary space. It had studio rooms for 10 young people and over the years it has provided a transition space for hundreds of young people.

By this stage Gordon had lost faith in the third sector, which he found unbusinesslike, relying on donations and paying workers too little for playing such an important role in society. He decided to get into property development. In his words he became *"the personification of Thatcherism, with a Penthouse apartment in South Kensington and driving a Porsche."* He played the stock market and lost heavily. By this stage interest rates had reached 18% so Gordon spiralled into debt. His lifestyle had become unsustainable and in 1992 he became insolvent. His mother had also recently died and this had a big impact on him. *"I felt in the past six years I had lost myself and money and status had become all-important. I needed to re-orient myself. I went into a time of deep self-reflection and put a back pack on and travelled for six months. Whereas life had been black and white, I needed to discover grey again, the contradictions that make me who I am."*

When he returned home, he started with a blank sheet of paper. At the time Michael Jackson had launched his "Heal the World" foundation and was looking for a CEO. Gordon applied and was rejected, but as he very rarely takes "no" for an answer he decided to call again, pretending that he had just seen the post advertised. He asked if he could still apply after the closing date and they said yes. From 250 applications he was shortlisted to the top three. Yet just before he was about to be interviewed, he was told that the head-hunter had recognized that he had already been rejected earlier and that no interview would take place. *"I felt utterly dejected. I remember walking behind Cleveland Square near John Lewis in Central London. My pace became quicker, then I stopped. It felt time stood still and I said to myself 'Fuck it, I'll form my own charity'."*

Gordon set about creating a business model that had social impact and was profitable and sustainable. This was long before the term "social enterprise" was in common use. In 1995 he founded "Training for Life," which took disused spaces and turned them into places of education and training for disadvantaged young people.

After the closure of "Training for Life," he took another period of time out, this time in Italy, where he bought a disused convent and turned it into a space of renewal, rest and personal wellbeing, called "Legacy Casa Residencia." It is there that Gordon brings groups of executives together to discuss issues that can address society's needs.

"I truly believe that to tackle the wider challenges we face in business, academia and government we have to work together and to recognize that social impact makes good business sense. Sometimes I ask myself 'Why am I doing this?' My answer is always 'Why not? It is needed and no one else is doing this right now'."

Rather than go into resignation and defeat, Gordon saw the possibility that arose out of rejection and failure. His "why not?" attitude gave him the courage to act in spite of not knowing what lay ahead.

10.

TAKE RESPONSIBILITY

When her organization went through a massive restructuring, throwing many people into the unknown, Jennifer Gale,[103] Director of Technology at an international financial institution, took matters into her own hands. It was 2011 and like most international organizations, the repercussions and impact of the 2008 economic crisis were still being felt in various pockets across the corporate world. Companies were reducing staff and very little hiring was taking place. Making the required cost savings meant making an ongoing review of resource profiles and re-evaluation of necessary deliverables. Jennifer had been offered a new role within the organization, but found out that the team she used to manage were going to be affected by the cost reductions.

Jennifer had spent many years investing in this pool of talented people. She worked with them to help develop their professional skills and broaden their experience. She also watched them meet their partners, start families and establish their roots on foreign shores. She found the experience of seeing their roles at risk very distressing, considering their skills, contribution and commitment to the organization.

"Then comes the choice: do I accept the top-down remit to reduce costs by approximately $1 million or do I explore all avenues to see what can be done to avoid loss of jobs and subsequent impact on these people's lives?"

It could have been very easy for Jennifer to brush this off as not being her problem. It was no longer her team and it wasn't her budget to protect. She remembers the exact moment when she decided that she was not going to sit back without doing anything.

"Sitting there staring at my computer, in complete anguish about the challenge put before us, in a single moment I decided that I could not live with myself knowing what was going to happen to these people without having tried to do something to help them retain employment."

With this newfound focus and energy, Jennifer took to her contacts. One by one, in alphabetical order, she systematically went through the list emailing, instant messaging and phoning them, asking if they had any open roles for some top-quality, experienced resources. To her surprise, her network of people pulled through. Jennifer started setting up interviews with hiring managers in parallel to talking to the candidates about the new opportunities. *"It was protocol to not indicate that their roles were at risk, so I was forced to rely completely on my influencing skills, encouraging them to be open to interviewing about new potential opportunities for their careers. Then taking a risk by not knowing the outcomes that were to follow, if they refused this new role presented to them."*

One week later, working across many areas of the company, having identified strong candidates that met the requirements of the hiring teams, 25 people were secured new roles in exciting new opportunities that were going to help develop their careers. The budget targets were also met.

"The choice to take responsibility not only made a huge difference to 25 people's lives, it made a significant difference to mine for knowing I did the right thing!"

DELIGHT IN THE UNKNOWN

CHAPTER 9

"We have learned that the past will be a poor guide to the future and that we shall forever be dealing with unanticipated events. Given that scenario, organizations will need individuals who delight in the unknown."

Business thinker and author Charles Handy

1.

FOOLISHNESS AND PLAY

*"The fool doth think he is wise,
but the wise man knows himself to be
a fool."*

William Shakespeare

To make decisions when we don't know the answer is surely foolish, yet sometimes we have to act the Fool. In Tarot cards, the Fool is traditionally depicted as being someone who is walking towards the edge of a cliff, and is about to step off. He carries a bag with all the possessions that he might need for the journey. He holds a flower, representing an appreciation of beauty, and a staff, a reliable tool for the journey. He faces northwest – the direction of the unknown.

The Fool is an archetype that represents all possibility and therefore it is an image for fluidity and flexibility. The Fool is restless but wise and he doesn't sit on his laurels. He is an adventurer, a wanderer, he knows when it's the right time to move and when to camp out, but he doesn't know where to go. His character is childlike, open, honest and unconscious; and we can think of him as a free spirit, following nature rather than a pre-planned path. He would be called "naïve" in our modern-day world. The late British painter Cecil Collins describes the Fool as *."..the* *essential poetic integrity of life itself, clear and naked, overflowing in cosmic fun; not the product of intellectual achievement, but a creation of the culture of the heart. A culture of the genius of life.*"[104]

The Fool's main message is that over-cautiousness is not good. He asks us to take a leap of faith and to trust in the journey. As Steve Jobs encouraged the graduating class of 2005 at Stanford University: *"Stay hungry. Stay foolish."*

For Rajeeb Dey, the CEO of Enternships, the youngest member of the World Economic Forum Young Global Leader cohort of 2012 and a co-founder of StartUp Britain, a campaign for entre-preneurship by entrepreneurs, foolishness was easier at the start of the journey. Now that he is an experienced entrepreneur, it takes more courage to step into the unknown. *"For me, it all start-ed with a problem that was bothering me. I didn't actually know it then, but that was the first itch of entrepreneurship – the fact that there was something wrong, and I wanted to know if I could fix it."*

Rajeeb was sitting in his bedroom in Oxford, trawling through the various job schemes open to him once university came to an end. Eyes glued to his laptop, the same words kept popping up in front of him: "accountancy," "consultancy," "law," "manage-ment." *"All gleaming, clear, success-ridden paths for people who knew that gleaming, clear, success-ridden life in a big company was for them. But I wasn't interested in being a small part of something very big. I wanted to set up on my own. Where was the path for that?"*

It occurred to Rajeeb that the local startups he'd dealt with as part of his extra-curricular passions were far more suited to people like himself – people who enjoyed the challenge of work-ing in small, agile teams, of making a difference from the start and of responsibility, accountability and passion. *"And surely a bright young startup needed bright young minds far more than the big companies did? It was annoying. It bothered me. Surely there was something I could do about it."*

The only thing he knew at that stage was that he wanted to take on this challenge. This turned out to be significant for Rajeeb. *"I think if I'd had any real idea about how much I was going to have to learn to get this problem solved, I would have been overwhelmed by the journey ahead of me. As it was, I was able to have a great sense of clarity from the outset."* The blank sense of unknown that lay ahead of him meant that he could keep the problem he was trying to solve at the forefront, at the centre of everything he wanted to do.

As a bright-eyed, naïve student, Rajeeb carried the fact that he didn't have all the information, finding his way as he went along, as an advantage. *"Going into something with a lot of unknowns makes you keep what you do know, the core of your mission, at the heart of everything. It keeps things clear."* At the same time, his journey to creating his startup Enternships would have been a lot more efficient, a lot less roundabout, had he known a few things at the start. *"My point is not to champion the blind leaping into a project without understanding how you're going to get started, far from it. It is simply that as entrepreneurs, as anyone starting out on a challenge that might seem large, it's important to find a way to free yourself from fear."*

Now Rajeeb no longer has the luxury of going into a project with the same glorious naïveté he had when he was a student. Sadly, he says, the freedom of leaping into the unknown isn't always appropriate. But, amongst all the shouting of the different responsibilities, of the tasks ahead and of the work to be done, he makes sure he keeps asking himself – "what if I didn't know any of this? What would remain? What problem am I trying to solve and why am I trying to solve it?" *"That still leads what I do, and I hope it always will. When I started out, the unknowns ahead of me make it easy to be brave, to take a leap. Now that the knowns have started to creep in, bravery can seem harder. But ultimately, it still comes down to clarity of mission, of those first couple of questions. Keep that at the front, and you can take on anything."*

2.

HUMOUR

Life at the edge can become very serious quickly, but this is quite natural. After all, facing the unknown through redundancy, illness or losing sleep due to a critical dilemma at work is no laughing matter. Yet paradoxically, humour and lightness may be just what's needed in the situation.

In the work context laughter is often portrayed as trivial, at best the consequence of banter and office humour, making the time go a little quicker. At worst it is seen as a silly, inappropriate escape from painful feelings and facing the "gravity" of a situation; certainly not fitting for the seriousness of business.

Joseph Geary, a positive psychologist from Dublin, decided that the best way for him to develop his humour was to train as a stand-up comedian. He distinguishes himself from the typical comedians, who are told from an early age that they're "naturally funny." *"I would like to make it clear that I was never told such things, but that will never stop me from making a fool out of myself. At least as a fool, I am honest."*

After a period of travelling, Joseph settled down in London and enrolled in a comedy school in Camden. On the first week, the students were asked to recount the most embarrassing experience of their lives. *"I recognized that this exercise would gauge how much we were willing to betray our ego in favour of honesty, in order to make people laugh. I was thrilled at first, as I felt that my own ego would be quite manageable (we Irish are trained to betray our ego from birth). I was confident that I would be able to dig deep and bare everything, metaphorically speaking in this instance."*

However, when it came to his first performance, Joseph felt his fear rise. He questioned whether the strangers in the class would hold his failure as lightly as he did. *"I began to recount a youthful escapade about how I 'half-lost' my virginity (I'll spare you the details and leave you in as much confusion as existed on the night in question). However, as I told my story to these strangers, I noticed that I detached from my feelings. I detached from their judgement and I saved my little ego."* What if the audience took him too seriously? Joseph wondered. Further, was it possible to live alongside people who took life too seriously? How could he help people see the funny side?

The course prompted a spiritual awakening (otherwise known as a "breakdown," says Joseph), which was made more severe when his comedy mentors asked him to think about everything he loved and hated in life. Again, Joseph recognized the call for him to expose his true self, his passions in life. *"And that was the key. For other people to see the funny side, I needed to be a 'verbal magician' and misdirect them with my passion. I was playing it cool and holding back how much I loved and hated the world because I didn't want the audience to get anxious, but that's exactly what's required! Being an 'average Joe' didn't stir them up enough."*

To live true to his purpose of "making the world feel good," Joseph realized that he needed to begin with his own vulnerabilities and anxieties. Making the audience anxious at the beginning would pave the way for laughter, he discovered. This view is supported by the false-alarm theory, proposed by neuroscientist VS Ramachandran. If we look to our primate cousins, they too get upset or confused, and consequently experience anxiety as they navigate their environment. When a chimp sees a snake and feels fear, they will shriek instinctively to warn others nearby, who then join in the shrieking to help raise the alarm. However, if the "snake" turns out to be a harmless stick, the chimp will laugh, and thus raise the "false-alarm" signal. Again, others nearby will join in the laughter to communicate that we all made a silly mistake. We laugh to communicate the very important message: "Don't Panic!"

"So when we feel afraid of the unknown, it's okay," Joseph reassures us. *"There's a punchline coming."*

Humour can defuse difficult situations and help overcome the negative and uncomfortable feelings arising at the edge. So rather than take things too seriously, we can take a leaf out of Joseph's book and turn the vulnerability and anxiety into a different story. One where we can laugh at ourselves and the situation and hold life lightly. This attitude is also embodied in the character of the clown.

A few years ago Annick Zinck, a leadership consultant based in Switzerland, completed an action research project into the intersection between play, clowning and leadership titled *What can Mr Leader learn from Mr Clown in unstable times?* The outcome was "Leadership Lab," a process bringing clown art and leadership together, that she developed with Tom Greder, a clown performing artist.

"The clown is comfortable with paradox and plays with ambiguity to create alternatives in the unknown. The clown practice is an opportunity to learn by doing, feeling and experimenting, as opposed to other more cognitive learning practices which dominate the world of work," says Annick. She argues that leaders who tend to look for technical, ready-made answers to complex problems can learn these skills by tapping into their childhood experiences and developing their own clown character.

3.
CURIOSITY AND CREATIVITY

"I have no special talent.
I am only passionately curious."

Albert Einstein

Maria Nekrassova, a Russian creative artist, entrepreneur and Associate Director of Admissions for a top European Business School that Steven coached, has made curiosity an everyday practice.

"5 am; I am standing in line in a Kazakhstan airport, tired after a business trip and bored. I start looking around not to fall asleep and notice a girl wearing a pair of high-heeled stilettos. I smile and think: high heels at 5 am? She must be Russian. I start amusing myself by looking at people's shoes and trying to guess where they come from. The guy next to her is wearing old-fashioned sneakers so loved by the Americans. I observe him for a bit then I notice next in the line a pair of soft suede moccasins, no socks. The temperature outside is -10°C and the style is unmistakable, so I smile when I hear Italian. I love the idea of having so many different styles standing in line so I secretly take a photo."

Maria spots curious situations, details, and things around her. To remember things better she takes a photo and saves it in a "Curious things" folder on her computer. It can be an ornament, an announcement or just a peculiar way the snow lies on the street. Sometimes when she notices things created by others, like the shadows of fences or buildings, she feels a strange connection with the architect, as if they shared the same secret.

Sometimes it is just life that brings up peculiar situations and angles in her path. *"I rarely feel that I create something, I just spot it. So I am a little bit ashamed when people tell me that I am creative. What I do is observe, not create, and anyone can do it. As Picasso put it, 'Good artists copy, great artists steal'. I edit my photos to make the idea clearer – I rearrange objects, crop a photo or use a filter, but the idea is never mine in a way, I just notice it."*

Maria's collection replenishes naturally. Her curious attitude originates in her belief in the world's potential affluence – the world has a lot to offer and there is always something to spot. *"My curiosity folder is not only a source of ideas. For me it is a constant reminder of how beautiful, funny and enriching the world around us is. It has so much to offer if you are eager to play and be ready to observe – most of the time just for the sake of appreciation and without any particular purpose in mind."*

Curiosity opens us to the world around us. It helps us see again with "fresh eyes" and allows us to make new connections that are crucial in working and being successful in the unknown. Beginner's mind is the key to creative work, as designer Benjamin Erben reminds us. *"As a communications person, a designer, almost every project I get myself into starts with an absolute blank sheet. More often than not I know nothing about my client's industry: insurance, music distribution, sugar industry, car safety systems, you name it… That is our strength. It's the fresh view we provide that's invaluable, and our confidence is contagious."*

AND VULNERABILITY

BOLDNESS

4.

BOLDNESS AND VULNERABILITY

"Freedom lies in being bold."

Poet Robert Frost

Opening up to the unknown requires boldness. "*Even though the future might not be clear, leaders still need to be bold in decision-making,*" argues Ben Hughes, Deputy CEO of the *Financial Times*. When the *FT* developed the FT.com app, it decided not to distribute the app through the Apple store. This decision was not made to avoid Apple's 30% cut of revenue but rather to ensure that the *FT* could own and control its own data. It was a bold move as Apple was dominant in the app space.

As a result the *FT* built its own app outside the Apple platform and made it available on the Android platform. It proved very successful. Ben believes that in the end Apple respected the *FT* for taking such a stand – it was a bold thing to do at the time.

"I think those in leadership need to model boldness in helping their staff to thrive while entering into the unknown. While I take wide counsel and absolutely seek advice on strategic or important decisions, once made I think you need to be confident and that

your body language also has to reflect this. This is particularly important in changing times."

Ben talks about the *FT* brand being a "confident" brand, not an "arrogant" brand. *"I remember when I first joined the* FT *over 25 years ago, then we were an opinionated brand. I saw the brand evolve to one of style and class, not arrogance. I think this takes boldness in decision-making."*

One way the *FT* embraced the recent uncertainty in the industry was to experiment with new streams of business. The *FT* leadership team needed to make bold decisions in changing the business and reducing circulation, even though they didn't know where this would lead. One example is the conference business, which was expanded and subsequently became very successful. The *FT* also acquired companies in the new digital and subscription space, such as Money Media and Executive Appointments. The luxury business was expanded, creating exclusive events such as the "Race to Monaco" which connected the readers in novel ways. This resulted in keeping advertising rates strong, even if print circulation had decreased.

One of the most inspiring speakers Ben has heard on going into the unknown was the mountain climber Joe Simpson, who was featured in the film *Touching the Void*. *"He faced a decision to climb up, or to go down into a crevice – down into the void. This bold decision to go down into the unknown may well have saved his life. I think as leaders we also face a choice, but that doing nothing or going back to business as usual is not an option."*

When Anna Simioni (whose story appears on page 59) received the feedback from her team, she was struck by how she was perceived – invincible, without doubts and fears, too independent and too self-confident. She realized that this image she had unconsciously created was disempowering to her staff and was getting in the way of them taking responsibility for their challenges and being able to thrive. She decided to create a workshop to discuss the data with them. By making herself the focus of the meeting and giving her staff the opportunity to discuss the data, she enabled people to begin to see her in a new light. That workshop was the beginning of a long, tough journey, where Anna started to drop the 'defence' of competence and control and enable her team to change roles. Seeing her in all her vulnerability and humanity facilitated their capacity to improve their competence.

"I cannot say that it was easy to make these changes. What was most difficult for me was the concept of vulnerability because at that time I felt I was strong and in a good place, not vulnerable. Initially, I felt that I needed to "play" vulnerable even though I did not feel this way. Over time since the survey, life has made me vulnerable. I now start to observe myself and notice when I am protecting myself, aiming to allow myself not to be shielded."

Anna displays a flexibility of character in line with Keats' "negative capability" in her ability to tolerate the loss of an important part of herself (the powerful, all-competent part) and the capacity to recreate herself as someone more open to Not Knowing.

Rather than seeing vulnerability as a weakness, it can be a source of strength and courage as we step into the unknown. A *Harvard Business Review* study shows that witnessing the courage of others embracing their vulnerability is inspiring and can have a positive "snowball" effect.[105] The study followed the managing director of a large German corporation who was struggling to change his directive leadership style. Instead of creating an illusion of invulnerability, he chose to acknowledge his current shortcomings. He stood up at an annual meeting of his top 60 managers and admitted he did not have all the answers, asking people to help him make the necessary changes.

Openly embracing his vulnerabilities was perceived as a respectable move of bold leadership by his team. Innovation and team initiative measurably increased and the company as a whole flourished as a result.[116]

These changes do not happen overnight, though. It may be hard to shake off the image others have of us and be perceived differently in a system, especially if those perceptions are entrenched. It is challenging changing roles when people's view of us is fixed. People will expect us to be predictable and behave as we've always behaved. Anna Simioni found that due to the historical legacy of her role, people still clung to their image of her, even when she changed her behaviour. It took her some time and persistence to re-establish her role as someone who shared power and worked collaboratively with others.

5.

COMPASSION AND EMPATHY

As we've seen, at the edge between the known and the unknown we come up against a myriad uncomfortable, unpleasant, and sometimes painful, feelings. Doubt, anxiety, anger and shame arise spontaneously and unexpectedly. The unknown questions and challenges our self-image of being competent and in control. Faced with our own incompetence, it is often easier to avoid the discomfort we are feeling than face an image of ourselves as deeply flawed human beings.

Becoming more aware of what happens to us at the edge enables us to become more accepting of the insecure, controlling, struggling or incompetent parts of ourselves – parts that we would rather avoid acknowledging, or pretend are not there. That awareness involves a deep and unconditional acceptance of our own weaknesses, failings and deficiencies; being at peace with ourselves and who we are, the whole of us, not just the parts that we like and that we are comfortable with. Experiencing those parts of ourselves that feel awkward, that are not fully known to us, requires an openness and generosity towards ourselves. It requires self-compassion.

Compassion is different from empathy. It goes beyond the capacity to put ourselves in other people's shoes to an active openness to our and others' feelings and experiences.

According to Buddhist teacher Pema Chödrön, *"Compassion is not a relationship between the healer and the wounded. It's a relationship between equals. Only when we know our own darkness well can we be present with the darkness of others. Compassion becomes real when we recognize our shared humanity."*[106]
Jeff Weiner, CEO of LinkedIn, is known to talk about com-

passion as the centrepiece of his management style. He describes how compassion requires slowing down and taking the time to truly listen to others. For him, being compassionate means understanding where people are coming from, and caring about the struggles they're facing and the baggage that they're carrying.

Steven: A few years ago I was doing a coaching programme where participants were asked what their life purpose was. Challenged by the magnitude of such a request to 'give my life purpose', I turned to my coach, who advised me to start much smaller and closer-in. Rather than a grandiose purpose, such as bringing love into the world, my purpose became 'to be a little kinder and more compassionate to myself when I struggle'. We can often be far harsher with ourselves than we would be with other people. Instead we can acknowledge that as human beings we are perfectly imperfect and cannot manage everything well, all of the time. Our challenge in self-compassion is to learn to be a better friend to ourselves.

The compassion we show for ourselves also allows us to be compassionate with others in their suffering. Everybody has their own challenges and struggles, of which we often know nothing. This idea was recently used in a film made by the world-famous hospital *The Cleveland Clinic*. The film explores how we would treat each other if only we knew what was happening for the other person, both good and bad.[107] This quality of empathy is a resource that enables us to connect, but can also lead to creativity and innovation as we understand the needs of others more clearly.

KNOWLEDGE
and
COMPETENCIES

LEARNING
and
CREATIVITY

SILENCE,
PATIENCE,
DOUBT
and
HUMILITY

6.

SOLIDARITY

"Let each of us lead a revolution of support in the lives of others."

Author and activist Bryant McGill

Sometimes we end up alone in the unknown, unable to share our fears, unable to talk about what's happening. We can be robbed of our voice at the edge, struggling to make sense of where we are and what is happening to us. Tanya Downs had always thought she knew where her life was heading. Then, at the end of 2009, she unexpectedly received the dreadful diagnosis of Multiple Sclerosis (MS).

"Previous to this I had been working full-on for a nice guy I affectionately call 'Captain Chaos'. It was an incredibly stressful environment, especially as three people had been made redundant and I was basically doing a three-person job on my own. Did I do well at it? I excelled in my role with Captain Chaos... even though I hated it. I was an avid cyclist and a heavy gym user, so I had a very active work and personal life."

Tanya's symptoms had started years before, with severe dizziness coupled with sickness, and pins and needles. It was only when she told her doctor that her pins and needles were spreading over her body that she was sent to a neurologist, who sent her off home with a very heavy dose of steroids. It was only when her eyes went "wonky" that Tanya was admitted into the neurological ward of St Georges Hospital in Tooting, London.

"I came back to my bed to a neat little folder entitled 'Information on Multiple Sclerosis for the Newly Diagnosed'. And then a locum doctor came up and confirmed I had MS. Everything I had been working towards suddenly was no longer an option or a consideration. Life changed with those few words in an instant."

She asked every neurologist she saw what her prognosis was, but nobody was able to give her an answer, or any indication about what her future held. Tanya felt mixed emotions, from relief that she finally had an answer to the strange symptoms she had been experiencing over the years to a resignation that she had a degenerative condition. She left her chaotic boss, removing herself from stressful situations and surrounding herself with positive people.

"My first MS nurse said to me when I was diagnosed 'Tanya, you will have to build your own support network', and I realized quite quickly that was exactly what I'd have to do."

Initially Tanya went onto the MS Society's website and chat forum, and discovered various pages on Facebook. After a while, though, she found these groups highly depressing and negative. Feeling that there had to be another way that women united with their condition and their own life experiences, and could converge and support each other, she decided to start her own network, "Ladies with Lesions" (LWL). The website and Facebook (private) group now boasts over 1,200 members in the UK alone. From that success she went on to start other support groups, including a support group for men (MiSters and Ladies with Lesions Together) and a group for family, friends and carers of MSers (Living with Lesions). The most popular and successful aspects of LWL have been the regional meets.

"Cakes, drinks and lots of laughs are standard issue at our meets. I have been all over the country, from Glasgow to Cardiff, to Southampton and of course my home London. Quite often I am struck by those who attend, who are generally housebound and quite lonely, who come out of their shells and enjoy our social occasions – I'm often told LWL has provided a lifeline for many of my members, and seeing the friendships formed has been super rewarding. One of our members also has our logo tattooed on her forearm – now that's dedication!"

Tanya is feeling proud and happy to have achieved something which benefits other MSers. The additional benefit is that she now also has somewhere she can turn when she needs support.

"My MS still troubles me, but I have a great medical team and am on medication to prolong my periods of remission. One thing I've come to realize through the past few years is that I used to be unsure of how uncertain the future would be. Now I'm sure of how uncertain it is. I don't know how I will fare in the future, but whilst sun is shining, I shall be making hay. That's all I can do."

There is an inherent loneliness in wandering in the wilderness and confusion of the unknown. But we don't have to do it alone. Whether we connect with others who are facing similar challenges or partner with colleagues to tackle a complex problem, we can be better prepared to face the unknown when we find our way forward together with others.

7.

FLUIDITY

"To go along with nature effortlessly, as does a fish or a master artisan, is to swim with the current, to let one's knife slip along with the grain. When nature is taken as a guide, a friend, living becomes almost effortless, tranquil, joyous even."

Author John Blofeld

DIANA: *Melbourne, 14 January 2014. It's 44°C (111°F) outside, the last of four days over 40°C. I am reminded of a day, almost five years ago, that is imprinted in the minds of many Australians, known as Black Saturday. The date 7 February 2009 marks the most devastating fire in Australia's history, with 173 people killed, 414 people injured, 2,100 homes destroyed, and 7,562 people displaced.[108]*

On Black Saturday, temperatures reached 46°C with winds in excess of 100km per hour. Approximately 400 bush fires started that day, many fed by winds in excess of 120km per hour, burning a total of 1,100,000 acres in the state of Victoria. The worst affected area was in the wooded hills northeast of Melbourne, known as the Kilmore East – Murrindindi area. There, some fires were reported to have travelled up to 600m per 30 seconds, the radiant heat capable of killing people 400m away. The fire was so fierce that trees combusted 200m ahead, and burning ember "bombs" could be shot up to 2km from the fire, starting other

fires. Scientists estimate that the energy released by the bush fires
was the equivalent of 1,500 Hiroshima atomic bombs.[109]

Stella Avramopolous had been in her job as the CEO of Kildonan UnitingCare, one of Australia's oldest community organizations dating back to 1881, less than five months when she found out about the catastrophic fires northeast of Melbourne on 7 February 2009. Her husband, a police officer, had heard the news on the police radio and had called her straight away. She dropped everything and headed to Kildonan's office in Whittlesea, on the outskirts of Melbourne, at the foot of the hills. There she gathered the team and set out for Kinglake, the epicentre of the disaster.

"At a time where there is something this big, clearly a crisis, you need to respond straight away. I had to see it firsthand because nobody had seen anything like this before. It was not normal business. I jumped in the car and went to assess the situation."

In the days after the fire had passed, services started to come into the area and community hubs were set up to provide emergency relief to the victims. When Stella arrived at Kinglake it was as if she'd landed in a war zone. People were running around, in panic mode. Everyone was coming to the community hub, the only community facility set up as an evacuation site.

"It was chaos, and I saw some crazy stuff. Clowns, people handing out bibles, Buddhists handing out money, radio stations setting up vans, banks setting up tents, Council members arguing with State government officials about who was running the centre. Community members were coming into the centre and were informed in front of everyone that their family had died."

Stella was there with Kildonan's grief and loss counsellor, Bernadette. She found a table and got two chairs and a manilla folder from the car. *"I wrote 'Counselling Support' on the folder and stuck it to the table. All of a sudden 50 people lined up. We took their name, number, any details they could give us, so we could start a database and talk to them."*

There and then they developed an intake and assessment system and slowed things down. *"When something that chaotic happens, you go back to basics – food, shelter, water, where are your family members... People wanted to be fed, clothed, have showers, talk about their family members who were missing... You just had to listen to what they needed, it was very concrete and immediate."*

At night Stella came down from the mountain and went back to the office. She sat down at a desk and formulated a strategic response on one sheet of paper, with objectives and timelines. There were three core things that she knew Kildonan had core capability in, which the organization could deliver: case management, financial counselling, and grief and loss counselling. The rest she left open. *"I left many question marks in there, as there were so many unknowns. We didn't know what was needed, and what would be needed going forward. We were living hour by hour, day by day. So we would have to adapt to the situation as it was changing."*

An added complication was the government's new "Bushfire Case Management Response," which Kildonan, like other agencies, had to put in place within weeks of the tragedy. Nobody knew what that meant or what shape it would take. In the three months that it took for the government to develop a manual, Kildonan had to develop its own response.

Stella knew that she couldn't throw the whole organization into the bush fire recovery response. Most services were delivered according to strict contracts with government departments. So she contacted the funders to see how she could use the funding creatively and flexibly. By day two she knew what she could adjust and what she couldn't.

Stella employed 20 new case managers, all recruited for a flexible attitude, open to dealing with a situation that nobody had encountered before. She also created a flat organizational structure to manage the new situation. Everyone from CEO downwards worked at the grass roots level, as the traditional hierarchy was no longer suitable. The flat structure and feedback loop meant the organizational response could be immediate. *"If one of my staff members had a meltdown at 11am, by lunchtime they would be back in the office. There was a worker there from another organization who was doing inappropriate things, and it took that organization three weeks to remove them. In a crisis, that response time is too long."*

New, devolved decision-making protocols enabled everyone in the organization, from the people sitting at the table in the community hub in Kinglake to the main office, to make decisions when confronted with unknown situations. This cut through the red tape, and freed up staff at the coalface to get the resources they needed.

Every action and every decision would refer back to the organization's shared approach:

• *Extraordinary times call for extraordinary measures*
• *The situation is new for everyone, so our response needs to reflect this*
• *Maintain strong partnership attitude, both internally and externally*
• *Maintain flexibility and respect for local community, maintain professionalism.*

Something new would happen every day, the situation sometimes changing overnight, so communication was crucial to keep everyone up to date. For the first three weeks Kildonan had two briefings, one at the start of the day and one in the afternoon. Stella kept the board members informed daily. They were naturally nervous about the new situation, so one day she took five members in the car with her to Kinglake, so they could witness the situation in person. Only by seeing it firsthand could they understand the sheer magnitude of the disaster, and Kildonan's approach. By then, 65% of the agency was involved in the crisis, with a 43% increase in staffing over a two-month period.

For the first three months Stella was very hands-on. She would often visit Kinglake daily, working side by side with her team.

"I had to care for the community and for my staff, from a close monitoring position. As we put processes in place I could gradually step back." Looking back over this period of time, she reflects: *"It was like being thrown off a plane without a parachute. It was so scary... I would arrive in Kinglake and have heart palpitations... it was overwhelming. But in the flight, you adapt by learning how to free-fall amongst the rush and the chaos... Actually, when you do that, it becomes very quiet and very organized and very clear. I quickly came to realize that I had to psychologically get myself in this space where I had embrace the chaos, and accept that I wouldn't and couldn't know what will happen. This freed me up to be present and respond to what was happening in the moment. Ultimately I had faith in the capabilities of the organization."*

Amidst the chaos and confusion, Stella led Kildonan through a reflexive, adaptive and holistic approach. Rather than fight against what was happening, or try to control the unpredictable and complex, the organization stayed nimble to the changing circumstances, providing crucial support and services to many families affected by the fires.

8.

ANTIFRAGILITY

'If you can force your heart and nerve and sinew, to do their turn long after you are gone, and so hold on when there is nothing left in you, except the will that says to them HOLD ON."

Author Rudyard Kipling

When Jon White stood on a bomb in Afghanistan, he had no choice about how many limbs he would lose – the bomb chose three. Both legs above the knee and his right arm at the elbow. The one thing Jon did choose in that moment was to "hold on," hold on to life. When the femoral artery is severed there is literally a three-minute window to stem the flow of blood before death takes place. It took his colleagues two minutes to find him and clear a safe passage to him so that they could perform the life-saving first aid.

0540hrs Wed 16 June 2010, Sangin, Helmand, Afghanistan
"'Buck, come on with me, make sure they put me to sleep, please Buck'. 'I will, don't worry Jon, you're doing well'. He places one of his huge hands on my shoulder, I needed the Sergeant Major there. The Chinook lands, I feel a little relief, I'm desperate, the deep burning throb of the tourniquets is more than I can bear, the guys start racing me to the open door, I can't remember who is carrying the stretcher. I'm inside, I reach out and grab a man

*in a flight helmet. 'Put me to sleep, put me to fucking sleep now'!
My head tilts to the right as the Chinook takes off, I see the ground
move out of the window and I relax."*

Sun 20 June 2010, Birmingham, UK

*"There's light, bright light, some moving colours and voices, I'm
sure they are voices. Suddenly there is clarity, my Dad and my
sister are at the end of my bed.
'We need to let Bex know what's happened, I can remember her
address Dad, get a pen and paper'.
'I can do better than that'. He leaves the room, the next thing I
remember Bex walks in, I've missed her so much. She makes her
way to the left of me and leans over, her head close to mine, she
tells me: 'It's ok, I'm not going anywhere, I'm going to stay with
you no matter what'. 'Well, in that case we should get married'.
'Ok, yes'. I remember her hugging me, I don't know how accurate
this memory is, or any of the above for that matter, it's all a bit
hazy now. Trauma and morphine does that to you."*

This was four days after the explosion. Jon found himself in
the newly opened Intensive Care Unit at The Queen Elizabeth
Hospital in Birmingham and he knew he was lucky to have survived.

The next few days are all hazy. He remembers being fed greasy
lasagne and chips, which made him sick. He remembers being
transferred off Intensive Care and onto Ward D. He was sick
again after they inserted a PICC line. At first he could not even
roll over, but gradually the pain resided and he was able to do
more and more. Jon remembers when they unwrapped his legs
for the first time. He had expected to see a patchwork of sewn-
up skin, maybe with a few scabs. What he saw instead was what
can only be described as two raw joints of beef. He almost cried
with the shock. Bex told him it was OK, it was normal and what
she had expected. *"She lied well, it comforted me,"* he says.

Jon made his decision quickly. He narrowed his options down
to two – *"Roll over and die,"* or *"Get up and get on with life."*

He chose the latter and started physiotherapy. Bex bought him a child's handwriting book as he'd had lost his right, dominant arm. Once he could climb into his wheelchair alone, Jon made a point of getting out of bed every morning after breakfast, dressing, making his bed and doing some writing practice before visitors arrived.

After his second week on the ward, a young plastic surgeon, Anton, told Jon that his legs were healing well and he could get out of hospital in two weeks' time. Jon hung on to this and the following week he told the consultant that he only had one more week before he was discharged. The consultant laughed and said his spirit was commendable. Luckily Jon knew the Ward Registrar, Sandy, whose brother had been the Medical Officer for the unit he had been serving with. Jon spent the whole week telling Sandy and the ward nurses that he was being discharged. By the following week's ward round Jon made sure he had all his papers in order. When he told the consultant he only had one night left, the consultant went along with it.

"I left hospital after 27 nights with both my legs amputated above the knee and my right arm amputated at the elbow. A true example of a self-fulfilling prophecy. If you have a vision and you communicate its certainty with everyone you meet, then it will come true. This is every leader's greatest tool, tell them there is a light, show it to them, even if it's just in their imagination, and they will follow you to the end of the tunnel."

Jon has not only survived but thrived as a result of his ordeal. He embodies what philosopher Nassim Nicholas Taleb calls "antifragility." Taleb describes antifragility as *"beyond resilience or robustness. The resilient resists shocks and stays the same; the antifragile gets better."*[110]

Under the trauma of his experience, Jon grew stronger. One year and three days later he hung up his wheelchair and has not used it since. He has learnt to walk, run, snowboard, kayak and drive a normal car, unaided and unadapted. He has married and become a father, built a "Grand Designs" home, and started a property development business.

The airline industry was one of the worst-hit sectors after the September 11 attacks, with drastic falls in passenger numbers resulting in plummeting shares and huge financial losses. Over the ensuing days and weeks, all American airlines cut jobs, with a total of over 140,000 people losing their jobs. One airline stood out amongst the rest by defying the trend. On 8 October 2001 Jim Parker, the then CEO of Southwest Airlines, made a surprising statement – *"We are willing to suffer some damage, even to our stock price, to protect the jobs of our people."*[111] The airline embarked on an explicit no-lay-offs strategy, which dismayed industry experts. Research carried out over the three years following September 11 studying the 10 largest US airline companies shows that Southwest was the only American airline to make a profit in every single quarter of the period studied. US Airways, which carried out the largest lay-offs of all (25%), followed the opposite trend, making a loss in every single quarter.[112]

The research shows that one of the key factors that accounted for Southwest's recovery from the industry crisis was its unequivocal commitment to its employees. In spite of the crisis and calls to follow the trend set by other airlines, Southwest remained true to its people-centred management philosophy and held onto its most important asset – the heart of the organization.

Rather than crumble under the shock of the crisis, the airline created strong relational reserves, which enabled it to thrive, a perfect example of anti-fragility. As an airline analyst remarked: *"They are doing what they do best, which is to shine in the hours of trouble."*

FINAL WORDS

THE GIFT

As we come to the end of our journey together, do you remember the beautifully wrapped gift you received at the start of the book? What did you decide to do – open it or leave it wrapped?

In the Ancient Greek myth of Psyche and Eros, Psyche is given several impossible tasks by Aphrodite. If she completes them, she is allowed to be reunited with her lover, Eros. Psyche's last trial is to descend into the Underworld and to request a perfume box from Persephone, Queen of the Underworld, which holds the secret to her beauty. This was no small feat as very few people returned from the Underworld. Psyche convinces Persephone to give her the box. There is one condition, though - she must not open it. Even though Psyche is told not to open the box she is unable to live with the mystery – she can't resist, she must know the secret inside. On her way back from the Underworld, she opens the box. As she does, she falls unconscious.

Regardless of the effect of opening the box, Psyche's story demonstrates how powerful our desire to know is. It can even overtake our reason and cause us grief. It is a reminder of the powerful force we have to contend with when we engage with Not Knowing. The question for us is, how do we react to Not Knowing? Do we accept it, engage with it, and make the most of it? Sometimes there is more value in sitting with Not Knowing - in leaving the gift wrapped.

Not Knowing may seem hard to bear. It can feel heavy, leaving us with worries and uncertainties. Yet perhaps it is also a gift that the all-knowing gods envied. To be human is to live with mystery, with the unknown. We are blessed with the gifts of curiosity, wonder, excitement and possibility. Perhaps in the end we will discover that this is the real gift of Not Knowing.

"It may be that when we no longer know what to do
we have come to our real work,
and that when we no longer know which way to go
we have come to our real journey.
The mind that is not baffled is not employed.
The impeded stream is the one that sings."

Wendell Barry, The Real Work

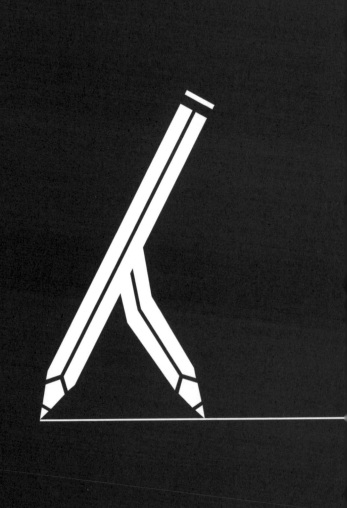

THE PATH IS MADE BY WALKING

APPENDIX

"I WOULD LIKE TO BEG YOU DEAR SIR, AS WELL AS I CAN, TO HAVE PATIENCE WITH EVERYTHING UNRESOLVED IN YOUR HEART AND TO TRY TO LOVE THE QUESTIONS THEMSELVES AS IF THEY WERE LOCKED ROOMS OR BOOKS WRITTEN IN A VERY FOREIGN LANGUAGE. DON'T SEARCH FOR THE ANSWERS, WHICH COULD NOT BE GIVEN TO YOU NOW, BECAUSE YOU WOULD NOT BE ABLE TO LIVE THEM".

Rainer Maria Rilke in Letters to a Young Poet

1.

LIVE THE QUESTIONS

In the spirit of Rilke, we would like to finish this book by inviting you to consider questions to live by and experiments to try. We would like to encourage you not to search for answers; not yet anyway. Instead, we encourage you to create the space for stillness, inquiry and reflection; to further build your capacity to become more present to the uncertainties and doubts that face you in your life and work; to build your tolerance to the uncomfortable feelings that arise at the edge of your competence; to create a new way, your way, of positively engaging with Not Knowing. As Rilke says, *"the point is to live everything. Live the questions now. Perhaps then, someday far in the future, you will gradually, without even noticing it, live your way into the answer."*

Questions are a powerful way to uncover new possibilities. They help us tap into our own wisdom and approach our lives with curiosity and wonder. Questions help us develop a positive orientation towards the unknown.

We offer the questions below as a starting point in your own journey, a portal to finding your own way forward. Allow yourself to live the questions that you feel most drawn to. If the temptation to think too deeply arises and you find yourself compelled to work out an answer in your head, try instead to hold each question a bit longer than you normally would. This may result in you expressing what you already know with a little freshness or newness, or it may create the space for new insights.

Alternatively, you could answer the questions without thinking deeply, going with your first response and following whatever comes up. Go with that, even if it doesn't seem to be what you "intended" to respond with, what you "should" say or what makes "sense." Also check in with your body. What sensations and somatic experiences do you notice? Whatever your answer, assume it is not the final answer, just like in a game show. You can continue to live the question and reflect on the question in your daily life.

To work with questions more effectively it helps to limit the time you have to respond. For example, you could begin writing as soon as you read the question. If somebody is reading the question to you, you could respond immediately with your thoughts. The key is not to "over think" but to limit the response time to one or two minutes maximum. Detailed plans are not needed from the outset. The point here is that you are not analyzing the question but allowing a response to emerge naturally. You allow the genesis of new thinking to emerge, from a place of Not Knowing.

You might also choose to live a question for a day, for a week, or for a longer period of time as a practice of inquiry. Some questions such as "What is my purpose?" are often revisited many times during our lives and the answer can change as often as we do.

Allowing a period for incubation can provide the opportunity to engage with what is happening around and within you as further data to draw on. For example, going into nature with your question and perhaps picking up an object that draws your attention may give you surprising insights into the question. Metaphors, drawing, music and other nonverbal ways to play with the question are all suitable. Sharing your thoughts with others close to you such as friends, family, a book group, or on social media, can provide support and add further wisdom. Find a way that works best for you.

No matter what you do, the most important part of the practice is for the question to remain alive, for your whole body and mind to become a question, suggests Zen teacher Martine Batchelor. *"In Zen they say that you have to ask with the pores of your skin and the marrow of your bones."*

On Knowledge

What is your relationship to knowledge? How important is it for you to be seen as competent in what you do? How does your specialty/expertise help or hinder you?

Have you experienced pressure in your role at work or at home to provide direction, clarity, certainty? How do you manage the expectations others have on you?

What is your own relationship to people in positions of authority? Do you feel comfortable questioning or saying "no" to authority?

How do volatility, uncertainty, complexity and ambiguity affect your role or context?

....

....

....

....

....

....

....

The Edge

What are some of your typical reactions when you arrive at the edge of your knowledge and expertise?

Where in your life do you employ a fixed mindset?
What would you begin doing if you did not fear looking, or being, incompetent?

What are some of the ways your resistance shows up when you are at the edge?

What is it that you long for? Where do you feel discontent or the call for something new?

....

....

....

....

....

....

....

....

....

Empty Your Cup

What are your personal or organizational values and how could you use them as your foundation for venturing into the unknown?

What does "letting go" mean for you? Who are the people who hold your safety ropes and how will they know to support you?

When was the last time you said "I don't know?" Where could you start adopting a "beginner's mind?"

What would be a safe context in which you could practise expressing "decent doubt?"

....

....

....

....

....

....

....

....

....

....

Close Your Eyes to See

What might you "close" to enable new possible ways of "seeing" to emerge?

How do you find space to listen to your inner voice?

What do you need to do to see something familiar and look at it with fresh eyes?

How might you work more explicitly with the assumptions you hold and test whether they are true?

....

....

....

....

....

....

....

....

....

....

Leap in the Dark

What are the structures you need to put in place to create the space for improvisation?

What are some of the complex issues you are facing that would benefit from generating multiple hypotheses?

How might you draw upon what you already have at your disposal to "tinker" or experiment with?

What role do mistakes play in your life? Are there contexts where you could embrace mistakes and failures as opportunities for learning and growth?

....

....

....

....

....

....

....

....

....

....

Delight in the Unknown

When in your life have you taken a "leap of faith?"

What are some ways for you to increase your sense of levity and lightness?

Where in your life can vulnerability become a strength? What would make it safer for others to disclose vulnerability in your workplace?

How might you show more compassion to yourself and others when facing the unknown?

....

....

....

....

....

....

....

....

....

2.

EXPERIMENT

When we are faced with a complex problem or situation, we don't need to know every step we are going to take from the outset. Instead, we can develop the experimental skill set of the scientist and the mindset of the anthropologist. The scientist devises experiments that test multiple hypotheses, shares results, looks for patterns and is open to alternative explanations.

The anthropologist has a keen awareness of all that happens around them and is highly attentive. They are not a detached observer but are aware of their own biases, and the biases of others.

Below we suggest some experiments for you to try, categorized under the main four themes of Not Knowing – "empty your cup," "close your eyes to see," "leap in the dark" and "delight in the unknown." If you try one of the experiments, take some time to review your experience. A journal to make notes may be helpful. In our experience, repeating an experiment that made no impact the first time may have a profound effect if tried again. Repetition can increase depth and resonance. Sometimes it is only repeated practice that leads to a new insight or mastery.

Above all, we hope you enjoy these suggestions. Play and lightness are often the best ways to learn something new. You can also devise your own experiments and adapt them to suit your circumstances.

Empty Your Cup
Teach first
A good way to develop "beginner's mind" is to speak about or teach something you are good at to someone who does not know anything about it. This may be someone in your organization, an apprentice or even a friend. For the brave, offering to teach or speak in a school or youth club is a good option. Children rarely hold back with their honest feedback. This experiment will allow you to see if you tend to use jargon and will force you to speak simply. It may also enable you to revisit the familiar and see some aspects that are no longer useful.

Making space
Letting go of physical clutter can also symbolically make room for mental clarity and space. It also serves as a metaphor for how much stuff we have that is not used or useful (beliefs, assumptions) and that by removing the old we make space for the new. You could start small – choose a drawer, or a cupboard that you have not looked in for a while. As you go through things that you have not looked at in a long time and come across things that you have not used for more than 12 months and are not important – bin them! As the space becomes clear, notice how you feel mentally.

Socrates for the day
Socrates was famous for asking questions and declaring that he didn't know. Choose a low-risk situation (e.g. not your salary review) and experiment by not answering questions put to you immediately. Allow yourself a few seconds' pause to consider the question. Take the question in with a genuine feeling of "I don't know" and, if appropriate, allow yourself to experiment with actually saying "I don't know." A useful tip is to imagine the question as a piece of food. Rather than swallowing it immediately, take the time to chew it over. Explore its effect on you, your first thoughts, what you feel compelled to reply, any emotions or feelings that arise in the body. A few seconds may feel like a lifetime, but it is only a few seconds. This practice

will raise your awareness and create the space for reflection and observation. It may also help you not to jump into action straight away.

All tied up

Many of us are creatures of habit. We perform many of our day-to-day routines unconsciously, with little awareness. From brushing our teeth to driving to work, often our attention is elsewhere. This experiment involves doing something very familiar in a completely different way. For example, you may try to put on your jacket the exact opposite way of what you would normally do. If your right arm usually goes in first, then use the left one instead. Tying your shoelaces the opposite way or crossing your arms and unfolding them with the opposite hand on top are other options. If there is a tendency to give up in frustration, persist. Notice how this feels. This practice will help you become aware of old habits and give you the choice of doing something different.

Close Your Eyes to See

Sound of silence

Silence is not simply the absence of noise, but a stillness that we can carry within us, to even the busiest marketplace. For one day, notice where you fill silence with noise and consciously choose to remain with the silence. For example, if you tend to turn on the radio in the morning while making breakfast, see what it feels like to do this in silence. If you normally have the TV in the background while reading or eating, turn it off. This experiment can strengthen the capacity to be with silence without reaching out to distraction, to be more aware of internal thoughts and chatter.

The world in your room

Choose a familiar place, a room in your home or a journey you routinely make (e.g. a walk to work). Imagine you are Sherlock Holmes surveying a crime scene, or an anthropologist observing the habitat of an unfamiliar community. Slowly and deliberately survey and pay attention to all that is around you. Notice the details, the textures and allow your focus to zoom in and out and really observe. Engage all your senses. The temptation is to bypass objects that are familiar, so take the attitude that everything is new to you. Notice how labels can get in the way of really paying attention to something exactly as it is without language. This experiment can sharpen the senses and develop the skills of observation.

Mind the gap

For one day in all your conversations practise listening fully and completely until the other person has finished what they are saying before making your point and responding. Notice any tendency to come in, or to evaluate and judge the content of the conversation. Practise holding attention completely on the other person. Be curious about their words, their tone, posture, facial expression. Notice the impact of the words on you, including any sensations that arise in the body. Deep listening creates a space of connection where ideas and possibilities flow easily.

Take three

We often forget to ask "Why?" and quickly go to "How?" Next time you are engaging with a complex issue, rather than jump into it, or take an approach that you've always taken before, see if you can ask "why?" with the curiosity of a three-year-old. If a "why" approach seems risky, you can moderate the question. For example, ask "Can you tell me more about?" This approach allows you to clarify the purpose and embark on the best course of action.

Leap in the Dark
There's an elephant in the room

Improvising your way forward means totally accepting what is being presented to you as an offer. It does not mean agreeing with it, but acknowledging and then working with it to go forward. For example, in improvisation sketches if one person says: "there's an elephant in the room," and the other replies

"No there isn't," the continuity ends. If the responder were to have accepted the offer and said "Yes, and the elephant is charging towards you!," we now have a sketch. With this in mind, think about what people say and do as an "offer." Take in what they have said with the "yes" of acceptance then build on their idea with your "and." This experiment can help develop a genuine creative dialogue in which both parties feel heard and can co-create something new.

Whose story is it anyway?
Choose an issue or a situation from your familiar environment and generate as many multiple hypotheses as you can about what might be going on. For example, you may see a couple at a restaurant. How did they come to be there? Are they brother and sister? Cousins? Is it a birthday or a secret rendezvous among lovers? Alternatively, take a situation at work. If you do this exercise with others, it can allow for more options to be generated. Think of hypotheses first alone, then group with others to avoid group-think. This process allows us to see a situation from multiple perspectives, and prevents us from jumping to conclusions too early.

90-day trial
An obstacle to change is the belief that something "just won't work." One way to challenge the killing of an idea too quickly, before it has the potential to succeed, is to do a 90-day trial. Choose a problem you are facing where there is some uncertainty around whether it can succeed. Launch a scaled version of the idea in a test for three months, without a commitment to continue unless it is a success. This approach removes the fear of trying something new as the option to go back to business as usual is still there. 90 days is just enough time to gain momentum and to allow a fair assessment to be made as to the idea's viability. Start to plan a low-cost, fast way to test the idea as a prototype. This experiment allows you to gain feedback fast and for bold ideas to be trialled without huge commitment or investment.

Different strokes

Think of a problem or challenge you are facing. Convene a group of people who have very different backgrounds and perspectives than you to talk about the problem together. It's not important they agree or come to a consensus, but that the differences are surfaced and everyone is given time to be heard respectfully. An alternative way to benefit from a diversity of opinion is to consider both sides of an issue that is being debated and to particularly show interest in a view that is the opposite of yours (e.g. if you like reading a liberal newspaper, read a conservative one). This experiment widens your perspective and challenges your own bias. It also develops the ability to hold two contradictory ideas at once and see the value of the argument in each.

Delight in the Unknown

Lighten up

Notice how your body is moving next time you are walking. Are your movements focused, tensed, rigid, or free and fluid? Notice if your jaw is clenched or relaxed. Allow your belly to soften. If you are at home, rather than taking a call or working sitting upright, experiment doing the same call with your feet up on a chair or the desk or lying down on the couch. When your body is relaxed it may also help your thinking become lighter. This exercise develops the capacity to increase our levity under pressure, making us more resilient. It can also give us perspective.

Secure base

Going through unknown situations can be emotionally exhausting. At times we need a secure base to which we can return, where we can be encouraged and find rest and the support to keep going. Identify who or what can provide a secure base to you. It may be a friend, a group, or a special location that has meaning for you. Practise going to this secure base (it can also be in your imagination) and notice how it supports you. How can you provide the same support for others?

Put away the sandpaper

Sometimes challenges that test our resolve can help us grow. Grit can produce character, forged under pressure. Yet in the unknown we can often face too much pressure and abrasive thoughts ("how did I get here?", "I should know better"). This experiment is about putting away the sandpaper and being kinder and more compassionate to yourself. For one day observe each time you have a thought of self-attack. Resolve to speak to yourself with more compassion. To be your own best friend.

ACKNOWLEDGEMENTS

Writing this book has been a true journey of engaging with Not Knowing – we experienced the initial tendency to rely on expertise, the struggle at the edge when faced with our own questions and doubts, and the surprising discovery of new spaces of learning and wonder. This experience provided rich insights that guided our exploration and writing. We overcame the challenges of collaborating across two different continents and time zones by finding our own rhythm, following the natural balance of night and day. As one of us would be collapsing exhausted in bed after a day's writing, the other would be waking up full of energy for the day's work ahead. We feel privileged for the chance meeting at Harvard Kennedy School in May 2012 that led to us working together on this book, and for the partnership that we have created.

We have been inspired by many writers, thought leaders and academics in writing this book. There are too many to list here, but we would like to especially mention the work of academics Robert French and Peter Simpson who applied the concept of "negative capability" to leadership; Marty Linsky and Ronald Heifetz, the creators of the Adaptive Leadership Model; Arnold Mindell, the founder of Process-Oriented Psychology; Otto Scharmer and the Presencing Institute; Byron Katie, founder of the "The Work"; and Fritz and Laura Perls, creators of Gestalt Psychotherapy.

This book would not have been possible without the contribution of the many people who generously shared with us their stories and advice over numerous conversations that sparked insight and supported the examples and case studies in this book. We could not include every idea or story in the book but we would like to sincerely acknowledge and thank everybody who contributed. If we have omitted anyone we ask forgiveness; it is not by design, and we thank you too for your support.

We would like to thank:
Eliat Aram, Marshall Arisman, Jean Claude Audergon, Arlene Audergon, Stella Avramopolous, Gina Badenoch, the late Alastair Bain, Anthony Ball, Paul Barber, Berrin Bas, Anna Beckman, Simon Berryman, Michelle Brailsford, Raisa Breslava, Christian Busch, Bruce "Harv" Busta, Michael Chaskalson, Michelle Chaso, Michael Cherock, Sherry Coutu, Michelle Crawford Sainsbury, Reka Czegledi-Brown, Niall and Elaine da Costa, Kito de Boer, Elitsa Dermendzhiskya, Teotonio de Souza, Rajeeb Dey, Julie Diamond, Tanya Downs, Simon D'Orsogna, Gordon D'Silva, Benjamin Erben, Maxime Fern, Danny Gal, Jennifer Garvey Berger and the Growth Edge Network, Nicola Gatti, Joseph Geary, David Hamilton, Charles and Liz Handy, Jane Harrison, Susan Hatch, Jennifer Hewit, Hans Hoppe, Ben Hughes, Master Ja An, Beth Jandernoa, Michael Johnstone, Ron Jungalwalla, Nassif Kazan, Peter King, Nicole Lessio, Robbie Macpherson, Karen Mahood, Julian Marwitz, Marco Antonio Martinez, Nadine McCarthy, Geoff Mendal, Jane Meredith, Megumi Miki, Deb Mills-Scofield, Maria Nekrassova, Suzana Nikiforova, Brigid Nossal, Simon Parke, Edurne Pasaban, David Pearl, Nicolas Petrovic, Joseph Pistrui, Anna Plotkina, Daniel Ramamoorthy, Samir Rath, Mobin Asghar Rana, Vicki Renner, José Keith Romero, Alex Sangster, Yvan Schaepman, Otto Scharmer, Alex Schlotterbeck, Aboodi Shabi, Anna Simioni, Liz Skelton, Terri Soller, Grant Soosalu, Carsten Sudhof, Jeremi Suri,

Nick Thorpe, Peter Tyler, Guy Vandevijvere, Tania van Megchelen, Rachael Vincent, Mark Walsh, Jon White, Randy White, Nick Williams, Jo Godfrey Wood, Chris Worman, Francisca Zanoguera, and Annick Zinck.

Thank you especially to Erin Smith for sharing with us her insights about vulnerability.

Thank you to Sarah Lloyd-Hughes for the metaphor of the present, which opened the book.

We would also like to thank Martin Liu, our publisher; David Woods, our editor; and the whole team at LID. We are grateful to Sally Averill for the introduction.

Thank you to Benjamin Erben, Nadine Rosenkranz, Maria Helena Toscano and the Iconic team for the inspiring artwork and design of the book, including the beautiful cover.

Thank you to Julia McCutchen, Director of International Association of Conscious & Creative Writers, our writing coach who helped us find our voice and stay motivated in the dark times.

A special thanks to Marty Linsky for his generous support and encouragement.

Steven

I want to thank my wonderful family, Silo, Christine, Selwyn and Charlene who are a constant support to me when I'm going into the unknown. When I fall, they pick me up and give me the encouragement to risk and grow.

I also want to thank: my mentor Joseph Pistrui who always sees possibility in me and opens my mind with his wit and wisdom; my Gestalt therapist Tommi Raissnen and my Gestalt teachers and training group members who have been my support in the times of anxiety that come with Not Knowing; and my teachers at Ashridge Business School and colleagues at IE Business School.

Special thanks to: Magdalena Bak-Maier, Kevin Coutinho, Matt Dean, Santiago Iniguez de Onzono, Marcus Docherty, Nicholas Frank, Anne Gabl, Sue Henley, Laura Hurmuz, Omar Ismail, Olivia Jamison, Nathan John, Gareth Jones, Dorota Juszkiewicz, Gulamabbas Lakha, Justine Lutterodt, Emma Pace, Ryan Pereira, Edina Szaszik, Jed Tai, Felix Valdivieso and Gerald West who all have played an important part in supporting this book.

Diana

I feel privileged to be part of the Adaptive Leadership and Process Oriented Psychology communities and thankful for all the rich experiences and learning.

Thank you to Meg Wheatley for the conversation in November 2013 which opened up a new door of inspiration and motivation.

I am grateful to Jane Martin, Process-Oriented psychologist and teacher, for her support and insightful feedback on the manuscript.

Above all, my deepest appreciation goes to my family; my husband Dale for discussing, brainstorming, challenging and improving my ideas; and my children Anica and Theo for being a reminder of all that is important in life – love, laughter and lots of questions.

ABOUT THE AUTHORS

Steven D'Souza

Steven D'Souza is a Director of Deeper Learning Ltd, based in London. He is an international executive educator, executive coach, speaker and author who has worked at the interface of leading business schools and corporations to design transformational learning interventions for senior executives.

He has had a diverse career from training as a priest, to becoming a Vice President in an investment bank before he was 30. He has has worked in the fields of HR, leadership and talent management, diversity, organisational development, recruitment and internal communications.

Keeping his links with industry, Steven brought his corporate experience into education, becoming an Executive Fellow for IE Business School (ranked #1 in Europe by the *Financial Times* 2013) in 2008 consulting on the design, content and experience of its international programmes. Steven has orchestrated its

Global Executive MBA as well as the Global Senior Management Programme, with Chicago Booth GSB. He has worked independently, from graduate to board level including CEO, with a firms such as Amex, Barclays, Credit Suisse, Eurostar, *Financial Times*, Goldman Sachs and PwC. He has also delivered workshops or talks for the United Nations ILO, On Purpose, the Hub Connections, TEDx and the Windsor Fellowship. He has spoken in places as diverse as Tbilisi, Bucharest, Shanghai and Sofia.

Steven has served on the guest faculty team of the Adaptive Leadership programme at the Harvard Kennedy School and is part of the Duke CE Global Educator Network (ranked #1 globally for Custom Exec Education by the Financial Times for the past 13 years). He has been a visiting lecturer on several programmes including at London Business School's EMBA, the Masters in Organisations and Governance at the London School of Economics, and the IE Brown Executive MBA. Steven has a BA (Hons) in Theology, Philosophy, Religious Studies with History and an MSc in Organisational Consulting from Ashridge Business School. He has also has studied Adaptive Leadership at the Harvard Kennedy School, Appreciative Inquiry with its founder David Cooperider at Case Western Reserve University and Theory U with Dr. Otto Scharmer from MIT.

Steven is also the author of three international bestselling books. He served as the Ambassador for the Australian Institute of Management and has been a co-chair of MERLIN (Business in the Community) and a Governor of the City of Westminster College. He has also directed programmes for the Windsor Fellowship educational charity.

He lives in London. He enjoys table tennis, nature, coffee and conversation, and exploring the relationships between psychology, philosophy, leadership, management and spirituality alongside social justice. He can be contacted at sdsouza@faculty.ie.edu

ABOUT THE AUTHORS

Diana Renner

Diana has spent most of her life moving from one state of Not Knowing to another. From fleeing her country of birth, Romania, to an unknown future in a new country; to a continuous process of professional reinvention covering the fields of law, strategy, communications, refugee advocacy and leadership development.

Diana is co-founder of Uncharted Leadership Institute, a global leadership consultancy focused on building the capability of organizations and individuals to successfully navigate complexity. In her work as a teacher, facilitator and consultant, Diana weaves together a range of disciplines including Adaptive Leadership, Complexity Theory, Adult Development and Process Oriented Psychology to help people become better leaders and make a positive impact in the world around them.

Driven by a passion to experiment with the ideas in this book, Diana has created Not Knowing Labs, immersive, interactive learning experiences designed to foster self-awareness, adaptability and creativity in ambiguity and uncertainty.

Diana has served as a Faculty member with Harvard University Kennedy School of Government for 'The Art & Practice of Leadership Development', The University of Adelaide and The University of Texas LBJ School of Government's 'Transformative Leadership Programs' and is a regular speaker and contributor at leadership conferences and events around the world.

Diana's passion for people, learning and creativity give her work meaning. She lives with her husband and two children in Melbourne, Australia.

www.unchartedleadership.com.au
www.NotKnowingLab.com

REFERENCES

[1] Feinstein, L, Sabates, R, Anderson, TM, Sorhaindo, A, Hammond, C, 'What are the effects of education on health?', *Measuring the effects of education on health and civic engagement: proceedings of the Copenhagen Symposium*, OECD 2006

[2] Taleb, NN, 2007, *The Black Swan: the rise of the highly improbable*, Random House

[3] Rock, D, 2009, *Your Brain at Work: Strategies for Overcoming Distraction, Regaining Focus, and Working Smarter All Day Long*, HarperBusiness

[4] Wolford, G, Miller MB, Gazzaniga, M, 2000, "The Left Hemisphere's Role in Hypothesis Formation", *The Journal of Neuroscience*

[5] O'Malley, CD, 1964, *Andreas Vesalius of Brussels 1514–1564*, Univ of California Press, p.74

[6] Bylebyl, JJ "The School of Padua: humanistic medicine in the 16th century" in Webster, C, ed., *Health, Medicine and Mortality in the Sixteenth Century*, 1979, chapter 10

[7] "Andreas Vesalius (1514–1564) The Fabric of the Human Body", Stanford University website viewed 10 March 2013 http://www.stanford.edu/class/history13/Readings/vesalius.htm

[8] O'Malley, CD, 1964, *Andreas Vesalius of Brussels 1514–1564*, Univ of California Press, p.98

[9] "Why are people overconfident so often? It's all about social status", *Haas Now news*, UC Berkeley, August 13, 2012, viewed 3 November 2013 http://newsroom.haas.berkeley.edu/research-news/why-are-people-overconfident-so-often-it%E2%80%99s-all-about-social-status

[10] Anderson C, Brion S, Moore DA, Kennedy JA, Mar 2012 "Statement Account of Overconfidence", *Journal of Personality and Social Psychology*

[11] Chamorro-Premuzic, T, 2013, *Confidence: Overcoming Low Self-Esteem, Insecurity and Self-Doubt*, Hudson Street Press, London

[12] 'Why are people overconfident so often? It's all about social status', *Haas Now news*, UC Berkeley, August 13, 2012, viewed 3 November 2013 http://newsroom.haas.berkeley.edu/research-news/why-are-people-overconfident-so-often-it%E2%80%99s-all-about-social-status

[13] Examples from Dunning D, Heath C, Suls J "Flawed Self-Assessment, Implications for Health, Education, and the Workplace", *Psychological Science in the Public Interest*, December 2004 vol. 5 no. 369-106

[14] Radzevick, JR & Moore, DA, 2011, "Competing to be certain (but wrong): Social pressure and over-precision in judgment", *Management Science*, 57(1), 93-106

[15] Grove, A, McLean B, "Taking on prostate cancer", Fortune Magazine, May 13, 1996, viewed 14 August 2013 http://money.cnn.com/magazines/fortune/fortune_archive/1996/05/13/212394/

[16] Tetlock PE, 2006, *Expert Political Judgment: How Good Is it? How Can We Know?*, Princeton University Press

[17] Heath C, Heath D, 'The curse of knowledge', *Harvard Business Review,* October 2006

[18] Ibid.

[19] Tversky, A & Kahneman, D, 1974, 'Judgment under uncertainty: Heuristics and biases', *Science*, 185, pp1124–1130.

[20] Zynga A, 2013, "The Innovator Who Knew Too Much", *HBR Blog Network*, April 29, viewed 22 August 2013 http://blogs.hbr.org/2013/04/the-innovator-who-knew-too-muc/

[21] Tetlock PE, 2006, *Expert Political Judgment: How Good Is it? How Can We Know?*, Princeton University Press

[22] Ibid.

[23] Schneider A & McCumber D, 2004, *An Air That Kills – How the Asbestos Poisoning of Libby, Montana, Uncovered a National Scandal*, Berkley Books, New York

[24] Goodman A, 2009, "Interview with Gayla Benefield", *Democracy Now*, April 22, viewed 22 May 2013 http://archive.is/XGNW

[25] Ibid, p.8

[26] Lee, S, 2004, "GROUND ZERO" Residents still counting costs of mining Zonolite Mountain, March 8, viewed 27 March 2013 http://www.greatfallstribune.com/news/stories/20040308/localnews/45266.html

[27] Hertz N, 2013, *Eyes Wide Open: How to Make Smart Decisions in a Confusing World*, William Collins

[28] British Academy Letter to Her Majesty the Queen of England, 22 July 2009, viewed 3 February 2013 http://www.euroresidentes.com/empresa_empresas/carta-reina.pdf

[29] Irwin N & Paley AR, 2008, "Greenspan Says He Was Wrong On Regulation", *Washington Post*, October 24, 2008

[30] World Chess Federation (FIDE) Ratings list viewed 17 March 2014 http://ratings.fide.com/download.phtml

[31] Gigerenzer, G, 2003, Conversations at the Edge, viewed 1 September 2013 http://www.edge.org/conversation/smart-heuristics-gerd-gigerenzer

[32] Gardner D, 2011, *Future Babble: Why Pundits are Hedgehogs and Foxes Know Best,* Plume

[33] Burton R, 2009, *On Being Certain*, St. Martin's Griffin

[34] Festinger L, 1957, *A Theory of Cognitive Dissonance*, Stanford: Stanford University

[35] Commission on Presidential Debates, September 30 2004, Debate Transcript viewed 17 March 2013 http://www.debates.org/index.php?page=september-30-2004-debate-transcript

[36] van Eemeren, FH & Benjamins, J, *Examining Argumentation in Context: Fifteen Studies on Strategic Maneuvering*, editors, John Publishing Company 2009, p.29

[37] Not his real name.

[38] BBC News Europe 2011, "Kaczynski air crash: Russia blames Polish pilot error", 12 January, viewed 10 October 2013 http://www.bbc.co.uk/news/world-europe-12170021

[39] Ackerlof GA, 2013, "The Cat in the Tree and Further Observations: Rethinking Macroeconomic Policy", iMFdirect, 1 May, viewed 3 June 2013 http://blog-imfdirect.imf.org/2013/05/01/the-cat-in-the-tree-and-further-observations-rethinking-macroeconomic-policy/

[40] Ibid.

[41] Ibid.

[42] Adams T, 2012, "This much I know: Daniel Kahneman" *The Guardian*, 8 July, viewed 13 July 2013 http://www.theguardian.com/science/2012/jul/08/this-much-i-know-daniel-kahneman

[43] BBC News Magazine 2013, "Hans Rosling: How Much Do You Know About the World?", 7 November, viewed 18 November 2013 http://www.bbc.com/news/magazine-24836917

[44] Kurzweil, R, 2002, "The Intelligent Universe", *Edge* Conversations 11 May, http://www.edge.org/conversation/the-intelligent-universe

[45] Snowden, D, 2012, "Cynefin: Revised Leadership Table", 1 Dec, Cognitive Edge Network Blog, viewed 10 January 2013 http://cognitive-edge.com/blog/entry/5802/cynefin-revised-leadership-table

[46] Snowden, D & Boone, M, 2007, "A Leader's Framework for Decision Making", *Harvard Business Review*, November, p.5

[47] Pillay SS, 2011, *Your Brain and Business: The Neuroscience of Great Leaders*, FT Press

[48] Langer, E 1975, "The Illusion of Control", *Journal of Personality and Social Psychology,* Vol.32, No.2, pp.311-328

[49] Thanks to Susan Hatch, Process Oriented Psychologist, for the notes on how to recognize an edge.

[50] Brown, B, 2012, *Daring Greatly: How The Courage to Be Vulnerable Transforms the Way We Live, Love, Parent and Lead*, Gotham

[51] Dweck, C, 2007, *Mindset: How We Can Learn to Fulfill Our Potential,* Ballantine Books

[52] Our summary from many interviews of people and clients about how they feel at the edge.

[53] Rock, D, 2009, "Managing with the Brain in Mind", *strategy + business* August 24, viewed 14 February 2014 http://www.strategy-business.com/article/09306?pg=all

[54] Chödrön, P, 2003, *Comfortable with Uncertainty: 108 Teachings on Cultivating Fearlessness and Compassion*, Shambhala Publications

[55] Not her real name.

[56] Fletcher, A, 2001, *The Art of Looking Sideways*, Phaidon Press

[57] "Burke and Wills' Fatal Error", Radio National Bush Telegraph, 7 August 2013, viewed 2 February 2014 http://www.abc.net.au/radionational/programs/bushtelegraph/burke-and-wills-fatal-error/4869904

[58] Ibid.

[59] Ibid.

[60] Harrison, D, 2013, "Annie King: more than a footnote in the mystery of the Burke and Wills expedition", *The Sydney Morning Herald*, viewed 3 February 2014 http://www.smh.com.au/national/annie-king-more-than-a-footnote-in-the-mystery-of-burke-and-wills-expedition-20130921-2u6fj.html

[61] Bion, W, 1980, *Bion in New York and São Paulo*. Strath Tay, Perthshire: Clunie Press, p.11

[62] "The Letters of John Keats: A Selection". Ed, R. Gittings. Oxford: Blackwell, 1970, p.43

[63] French, R, Simpson, P, Harvey C, "Negative Capability: A contribution to the understanding of creative leadership". In: Sievers, B, Brunning, H, De Gooijer, J and Gould L, eds. (2009) *Psychoanalytic Studies of Organizations: Contributions from the International Society for the Psychoanalytic Study of Organizations*, Karnac Books

[64] Ibid.

[65] Ibid.

[66] Yunnus, M, 2012, "One Young World 2012 Summit", viewed 25 January 2014 https://www.youtube.com/watch?v=USddwTvRdJc

[67] Ibid.

[68] Hlupic, V, 2001, "Increasing profits by giving up control", 21 November, viewed 10 March 2014 http://www.youtube.com/watch?v=4a0YxGC7auI

[69] Davis, J, 2013, "How a Radical New Teaching Method Could Unleash a Generation of Geniuses" 10 May, viewed 20 January 2014 http://www.wired.com/business/2013/10/free-thinkers/

[70] Kreider, T, 2013, "The Power of 'I don't know'", *New York Times, Opinionator*, April 29

[71] Simpson, PF, French, R, Harvey CE, 2002, "Leadership and negative capability", *Human Relations* 55; 1209; p.1211

[72] The Economist, 2013, "Bush's Legacy", Oct 26

[73] de Botton, A, 2002, *The Art of Travel*, Hamish Hamilton

[74] Wheatley, M, 2010, *Perseverance*, Berrett-Koehler Publishers

[75] Marvel MK, Epstein RM, Flowers K, Beckman HB, 1999, "Soliciting the patient's agenda: have we improved?" *JAMA* 281(3):283-287

[76] Scharmer, OC, 2007, *Theory U: Leading from the Future as It Emerges*, Cambridge, MA: Society for Organizational Learning

[77] Scharmer, OC, 2008, "Uncovering The Blind Spot of Leadership", *Leader to Leader* Vol. 2008, Issue 47, pp.52-59

[78] Ungunmerr-Baumann, M, Eureka Street TV, viewed 13 March 2014 https://www.youtube.com/watch?v=k2YMnmrmBg8

[79] Creative Spirits, "Deep Listening", viewed 15 March 2014 http://www.creativespirits.info/aboriginalculture/education/deep-listening-dadirri

[80] Joyce, P, Sills, C, 2010, *Skills in Gestalt Counselling & Psychotherapy*, Sage Publishing

[81] O'Malley, CD, 1964, *Andreas Vesalius of Brussels 1514–1564*, Univ of California Press

[82] Ibid. p.82

[83] Ibid. p.87

[84] Ibid.

[85] Batchelor, M, 2008 "What is This?", *Tricycle Magazine* Fall issue

[86] Bolte Medical website viewed 12 December 2013 www.boltemedical.com

[87] Intuit Network, 2011 "Leadership in an Agile Age", April 20, viewed 26 January 2014 http://network.intuit.com/2011/04/20/leadership-in-the-agile-age/

[88] Ibid.

[89] Eisenberg, B, 2013, "Leadership in the Age of Agility and Experimentation", Mar 22, viewed 26 January 2014 http://www.bryaneisenberg.com/leadership-in-the-age-of-agility-experimentation/

[90] Intuit Network, 2011, "Leadership in an Agile Age", April 20, viewed 26 January 2014 http://network.intuit.com/2011/04/20/leadership-in-the-agile-age/

[91] Wilson, I, 2012, "A hitchhiker's guide ...: Myersville man gives filmmaker John Waters a ride", *FrederickNewsPost.com*, May 24

[92] Rosen, J, 2012, "Baltimore Insider', *The Baltimore Sun*, May 22

[93] Itzkoff, D, 2012, "John Waters Tries Some Desperate Living on a Cross-Country Hitchhiking Odyssey". The New York Times, May 25, viewed 20 March 2014 http://artsbeat.blogs.nytimes.com/2012/05/25/john-waters-tries-some-desperate-living-on-a-cross-country-hitchhiking-odyssey/?_php=true&_type=blogs&_php=true&_type=blogs&_r=1

[94] Dunn, M, 2012 "Stepping into the unknown – adventurers working towards nailing extreme challenges like Felix Baumgartner", *Sunday Herald Sun,* Oct 28, viewed 29 July 2013 http://www.dailytelegraph.com.au/news/the-last-six-frontiers/story-e6freuy9-1226504379167

[95] "Works of Franklin D. Roosevelt, Address at Oglethorpe University, May 22, 1932", *New Deal Network*, viewed 10 December 2013 http://newdeal.feri.org/speeches/1932d.htm

[96] "Is this Obama's FDR style 'experiment' for our economy?" Klein Online, September 9, 2012, viewed 13 December 2013 http://kleinonline.wnd.com/2012/09/09/is-this-obamas-fdr-style-experiment-for-our-economy/#

[97] Miller, M, 1983, FDR: An Intimate History, Garden City, N.Y., p.263, quoted on http://georgiainfo.galileo.usg.edu/FDRarticle1.htm#anchor329597

[98] Singer, SJ & Edmondson, AC, 2006, "When Learning and Performance are at Odds: Confronting the Tension", p.10, viewed 3 February 2014 http://www.hbs.edu/faculty/Publication%20Files/07-032.pdf

[99] Ibid.

[100] Ibid. p.15

[101] Ibid.

[102] "The IDEO Difference", *Hemispheres, United Airlines*, Aug 2002, p.56

[103] Not her real name.

[104] Collins, C, 2002, *The Vision of the Fool and Other Writings*, Golgonooza Press

[105] Fuda, P & Badham, R, "Fire, Snowball, Mask, Movie: How Leaders Spark and Sustain Change", *Harvard Business Review*, Nov 2011

[106] Chödrön, P, 2002, *The Places That Scare You: A Guide to Fearlessness in Difficult Times*, Shambhala Classics

[107] The Cleveland Clinic http://www.youtube.com/watch?v=cDDWvj_q-o8

[108] Black Saturday Bushfires, viewed 20 December 2013 http://www.blacksaturdaybushfires.com.au/

[109] Ibid.

[110] Taleb, N, 2012, *Antifragile: Things That Gain from Disorder*, Random House

[111] Visser, C, 2005, "Organizational Resilience in Times of Crisis", viewed 29 December 2013 http://articlescoertvisser.blogspot.com.au/2007/11/organizational-resilience-in-times-of.html

[112] Ibid.

BEYOND THE WRITTEN WORD

AUTHORS WHO ARE EXPERTS

LID Speakers are proven leaders in current business thinking. Our experienced authors will help you create an engaging and thought-provoking event.

A speakers bureau that is backed up by the expertise of an established business book publisher.

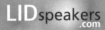